# NORTH DAKOTA CURIOUS:
## A NEW GUIDE TO THE STATE

## SYLVIA WENDEL

North Dakota Curious: A New Guide to the State

Copyright © 2014 Sylvia Wendel

Cover Image Courtesy of Valerie Root
Cover Design by Scott Carpenter
Interior Photos Copyright S. Wendel/I. Wendel,
unless otherwise specified.
Formatted by IRONHORSE Formatting

ISBN-13: 978-0615995328

# CONTENTS

# PART ONE – TRAVELING THE STATE

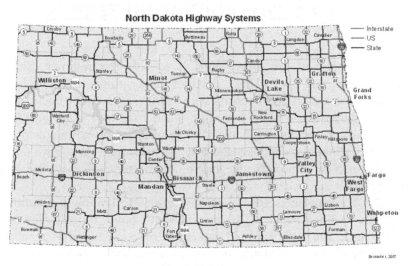

*North Dakota*

*Please note: We recommend you NOT rely on this or any other map in this book for navigation. You can obtain free maps through **www.ndtourism.org** or from your local AAA. Rand McNally and other companies offer maps for sale. **Do not depend on GPS**. It's often out of date or unreliable in rural areas.*
### map courtesy of dot.nd.gov

*North Dakota's Regions*

# WHY THIS BOOK IS DIFFERENT

We think you are smart enough to use the internet. Sites like *TripAdvisor* and *Yelp* offer detailed descriptions of lodgings and restaurants from five-star resorts with 9000 thread-count linens down to the last sheepwagon b&b located on a dirt road by the body shop. This book trusts its readers with the intelligence and discernment to choose their own dinners, breakfasts and beds for the night. When we provide a detailed review of a particular lodging or dining choice, it's because *we were there.*

This book respects sportsmen, but guides to fishing and hunting the state are in good supply. This book doesn't cover those topics. At any given time, the author would rather be on a hiking trail than almost anywhere else on the planet, but this is not a backpacking and camping guide. Those guides, too, are already available.

**This book is the only book that is completely about North Dakota**, the state, seen from a traveler's point of view. This is a guide for curious travelers, who want to know more about what they see than when is the next Taco John's. This book is for people independent and intrepid, curious people who don't travel to see theme parks or golf courses but who maintain a fascination with the rare and the unknown and who are always ready to, in Joseph Conrad's words, "Come and find out."

# INTRODUCTION
## WHY NORTH DAKOTA?

Because it's there. Because it's big, it's empty and it's beautiful. Because maybe you've forgotten the words to "America the Beautiful," especially the "amber waves of grain" part. Because maybe you think there's no romance, no innocence, no honesty and no absolute truth left in this country. Because part of you is aching for a place where the sky is entertainment, the ground is soft and yielding, the air is clean, the roads are good, and the people really, really glad to meet you.

Parts of it are flat. Most of it is farmland. Some of it is quaking underfoot as the biggest oil boom of the last hundred years continues to frack billions of dollars of black gold from the ground. Much of it is water, vigorous rivers and countless lakes, some round as dimes, some stretched-out and elongated like a Modigliani figure. Some of it looks like Arizona, other parts like northern Michigan. It is all beautiful.

Flat is beautiful. Farmland is beautiful. Farm equipment is beautiful. Step out of the car. Look at the fields. Feel the wind, the wind that never stops, trying to blow new ideas into your brain. Allow yourself to think. Not react, not comment, not joke, just think. Better yet, feel.

Do you let other people tell you what to like? Are you a clone or a robot? Is what's good enough for others good enough for you? If the answer is no – and it should be -- then come to visit North Dakota, because you will love the place.

Maybe your grandfather came from there. Or maybe his grandfather did, but either way you loved those stories about breaking ice to wash and walking five miles in a blizzard to school and what happened behind the tent at those springtime revival meetings.

Maybe your aunt was a barnstorming pilot or your uncle went to school with Roger Maris or your cousin has every record Peggy Lee ever made, or the old-age home where your kid does community service keeps playing those Lawrence Welk records and there's just something about that accordion that fetches you.

Do you like honey and herb tea? North Dakota makes those things.

Or perhaps you're looking to marry a millionaire, or become one yourself. The *Wall Street Journal* noted that more millionaires were created in North Dakota between 2012 and 2014 than in any other state. More than on Wall Street, more than in Silicon Valley. The stats speak for themselves.

For all these reasons and many more, North Dakota deserves your attention. Tourist dollars will go far. Gas, for example, was twenty to thirty cents cheaper in the summer of 2013 than on either coast. It's the rare hotel that charges more than $150 per night. Taxes are low, and real estate can be as cheap as the dirt under the foundations (Williston and environs are a notable exception, but we'll get to that). Restaurant meals are a bargain, although you'll have to work hard to avoid an overload of carbs and calories. If you don't gain weight on a trip to North Dakota, see your doctor.

Nothing to see? Nothing to do? The purpose of this guide is to **disprove preconceptions, smash the stereotypes** and show you, the traveler, a state with more variety and more new things to do than a dozen Disney Worlds. There's no admission fee to North Dakota, hardly any long lines even at the most popular attractions, no phony smiles and no plainclothes security talking into their lapels. This state is part of the free world.

Come in spring, when the snow melts and the trees are in flower. Come in fall, when purples, yellows, reds shine up the landscape. Come in summer, when warm winds turn the fields into rippling green seas. Come in winter if you dare, and join the icefishers, the snowmobilers, the skiers and the skaters, and all the folks indoors.

North Dakota is the real world, and its own world. Let it be part of yours.

*"Come and find out."*

4

# THE BEST OF NORTH DAKOTA
## BEST ROADS

There are no toll roads in North Dakota, which is good news for the traveler. **I-94** runs the full length of the state from east to west, while **I-25** hugs the Red and Sioux Rivers from north to south on the state's eastern end. That's not to say that everything else is rutted gravel, though, far from it. North Dakota contains some of the most interesting and least-traveled highways in the country.

We'll assume you're looking at a good, detailed map as you read this section.

### U.S. 83 – Border to Border

Among these is U.S. 83, a classic two-lane blacktop for most of its length, that runs all the way from Eagle Pass, Texas to the Canadian border, roughly paralleling the 100th parallel. This road is fascinating for several reasons. First of all, it basically bisects North Dakota, running right through the middle of the state, making it a good reference point for navigation. Then there's the interesting fact that east of here, the land is flatter and wetter (rainfall jumps by 15 inches once the 100th parallel is crossed), the farms raise wheat and corn, and the feel is more Minnesota than the Great Plains.

West of U.S. 83, farms become ranches and cattle is king. Wranglers replace overalls as everyday work wear, and the land is scarred – or improved, depending on your point of view – by erosion. In North Dakota, U.S. 83 is a four-lane highway from Bismarck (where it intersects I-25) to the Manitoba line, making it as fast as any interstate but far more interesting.

### U.S. 2 – The Great Northern Road

U.S. 2 enters the state at Grand Forks and exits it just west of Williston. This road gets started in Michigan's Upper Peninsula and winds its way across Wisconsin and Minnesota before crossing the Red River at the North Dakota line. West of here, U.S. 2 follows the railroad along the far-flung townlets of Montana's Hi-Line and the Idaho Panhandle before petering out at Spokane. This "ribbon of highway," in Woody Guthrie's phrase, takes motorists along some of the loneliest parts of America, as well as through the boomlands surrounding the Bakken

Shale.

You should be careful on U.S. 2 in and near Williston. Hulking semis haunt the lanes and everyone is in a hurry. Prepare to take your time.

## U.S. 52 – Slanting Sideways

This is a two-lane blacktop that goes to four lanes every once in a while (for example, near Jamestown). U.S. 52 is a diagonal, arrowing from Portal at the Canadian border down to I-94, where it merges with the Interstate to enter Minnesota. This road takes the traveler from northwest to southeast, through many rural North Dakota communities live, dead and moribund. The place names reflect the settlers' ethnic heritage: Voltaire (French), Bergen (Norwegian), Fessenden (German) and Anamoose, which sounds mysterious but is actually Native American. Route 52 is the best way from Minot to the southeast portion from the state, but its most interesting miles may be from Minot north, where it moseys along next to lakes, wildlife refuges, and the luminous hamlet of Lignite.

Also on Route 52: Velva, the home town of 1960s TV anchor Eric Sevareid, whose graying crew cut and competent demeanor graced the CBS evening news for years.

## N. D. 5 – Along the Top Edge

Curious travelers will love Route 5, as it leads to several big-time small-town curiosities: Bottineau's gigantic turtle on a snowmobile, Dunseith's giant turtle constructed entirely of wheels, a Stonehenge facsimile called "Mystical Horizons", and other honeywhat'sTHAT-evoking manifestations of the strange.

Two-lane all the way, Route 5 takes the traveler from the woods and rivers of Pembina all the way to the horizon-filling wheatfields surrounding Fortuna at the northwestern end of the state. Out there you'll find curling arenas, representing a south-of-the-border infiltration of Canada's other ice-rink sport. Winter Olympics junkies (this author is one) may want to wander in and throw a stone or two. Bring your own broom.

## U.S. 13 – Eastern Stars

You'll know **Route 13** by its distinctive sign, a large Indian head in profile. This two-laner runs in a mostly straight east-west line from Wahpeton in the far southeast to the Missouri River, where State Route 21 (see below) follows at approximately the same latitude. If Lawrence Welk had ever come home again, he would have needed Route 13 to get from Fargo to his family's old home near Strasburg.

## BEST ROADSIDE ART

In most states, you have to find your way to a museum or a gallery, drive and park or put up with public transportation, face long lines and crowds, just to see a work of art. On some North Dakota roads, however, all you have to do is slow down. The state abounds in fresh, original large-scale art installations erected in vacant fields and yours for the looking. Handmade but globally informed, these stylized interpretations of animals, insects and humans bring you new ways of looking at what you are seeing.

### Enchanted Highway

Take Exit 72 south off I-94 in the direction of Regent. You can't miss the exit – there's a flock of geese in flight rendered in metal over a sign advertising the drive.

Artist Gary Greff has spent twenty-five years designing, planning and building the set of six sculptures that line the sides of this particularly rural road. His distinctive big-eyed people and animals in characteristic attitudes rivet passers-by. who naturally want to know how-the-heck-did-he-build-that-anyway. Greff is also the proud record-holder of the World's Largest Scrap Metal Sculpture title, awarded by and mentioned in the Guinness Book of World Records (see **North Dakota Records**).

In 2012, Greff converted an old schoolhouse into an inn, the **Enchanted Castle** (563-4858). Statues of knights in armor greet guests, who can choose to soak in hot tubs in the former locker rooms or prepare food in their suites (all the rooms have kitchenettes). At the accompanying gift shop, there are all sorts of goodies including mini-sized replicas of the highway giants. Ask for Greef, since he's almost always around the property and ready to answer your questions.

## BEST URBAN SCENE

Sometimes only four blocks make a city. Sometimes just a few good stores, choice restaurants and friendly bars give a place that certain buzz. Whenever you're there, you're everywhere. At such times, and you will have them, don't forget: this *is* North Dakota!

**Fargo**, not surprisingly, takes this prize. Its compact, eminently walkable downtown offers a wide range of eating places and watering holes, along with one-of-a-kind shops, theatres and clubs. What we like about downtown Fargo is that it's also a practical place: you can buy daily or sometime necessities here, not just antiques and art. Croissants, yes, but also doughnuts and toothpaste. Add to this the presence of North Dakota State University only a few blocks north, and you've got a city center that meets the needs of all its citizens, not just a transient, affluent few.

**Devils Lake**, although much smaller, preserves its historic downtown and is almost always lively. Check out their webcam at **http://www.gondtc.com/webcam-main_street.html**: even when it's subzero and snowing, people are coming and going here, taking care of business, meeting friends, and having lunch. You'll feel warm inside.

## BEST SMALL TOWN ATMOSPHERE

It has to do with architecture, green space, historic role, variety and being able to walk or bike almost anywhere. It's not about what stores or which chain restaurants. It's about the football games, the bake sales, perhaps the annual Festival. It's about how you, the tourist, are treated when you step out of your shiny rental car, as obviously out of place as an elephant straight from Jaipur. These are the towns and villages that inspire those let's-buy-a-place-here conversations that are never entirely frivolous. These are the best small towns in a state with lots of them.

### Rutland
This was a difficult decision to make, partly because this book is partial to small towns and partly because there were just so many cool contenders. When all is said and done, however, Rutland in far southeast North Dakota ticks off the most boxes. Charming, yet functional; historic, yet not frozen in time; friendly, but not greedy. We've all been to towns that are long on aesthetics and local associations, but the only time you'll see a smile in those places is when they ask you, "Visa or Mastercard?" Rutland is not that place.

## BEST SCENERY

First, what kind of scenery are we talking about here? Is it the Badlands with their twisted trees, cannonball stones, and flaming red scoria cliffs? Or is it the lush, green, watery wonderland of the northeast, with meandering streams, hardwood forests and wide meadows? This is why there is always more than one best.

## Little Missouri State Park

On the edge of the Bakken oil shale, this place is a badland fancier's dream. The park's location on a high escarpment delivers panoramic views, while fields of sunflowers lead up to the park. While not as well-known or as visited, as Theodore Roosevelt National Park to the west and south, Little Missouri contains all the colors, shapes and contrasts of its bigger neighbor in one compact, manageable place. Please don't just drive in, snap some pix, and drive back out again; if you go, plan to stay for a while and ask a park ranger about hiking, horseback riding, and other ways to see this exceptional portion of the state.

## Gunlagson Nature Preserve

If scenery for you contains the color green, you'll want to tarry at the Gunlagson Nature Preserve at Icelandic State Park in northeast North Dakota. Water-loving plants like ferns and horsetails grow in great profusion here, and the fall color show shouldn't be missed. Hushed, untrammeled, full of variety and yet close to major highways, the **Gunlagson** provides a relaxation center for the stressed-out soul. The park is small, but the rewards can be enormous.

## BEST BAKKEN ESCAPE

## Lostwood National Wildlife Refuge

If you live there, you know: sometimes you need a break from the madness. If you're working in the oil patch, you can't do your best unless you repair what Williston does to your hearing, your allergies and your sanity. When you need your own personal breakout, head for Lostwood National Wildlife Refuge and the cluster of lakes that surround it. Mosquito Butte (bad name, nice place) rises from the prairie to 2300 feet, and the White Earth River to the west may tempt you to toss in a line and catch your dinner (check local regulations first). This is a great place to go when your brain feels coated with light sweet crude.

## BEST HISTORIC SITE

In a state where Lewis and Clark spent more time than anywhere else along their there-and-back-again coastal trek, there are bound to be myriads of duly noted historical sites. Meriwether and Bill, however, don't hold a monopoly in North Dakota, and there are many other places where the past lives again (or, more like it, has never gone away).

## Knife River Indian Villages and National Historic Site

One of the best is this mouthful, perched on the west side of the Missouri, just south of the "great bend" at Pick City. Not only did Lewis and Clark spend a winter around here, but Indian scholar and artist George Catlin visited in the 1830s, just before the horrible smallpox epidemic that shrank the Mandan tribe to almost nothing. Look up Catlin's paintings before you go, and see how easy it is to imagine their scenes – kids running, warriors boasting, young women chatting coyly among themselves, older women hauling and working – taking place in this area which, thankfully, has been left almost as it was over two hundred years ago. North Dakota winters are harsh, but step inside a Mandan earth lodge and you'll probably sense how inviting, spacious and even warm it could be when blizzards rage outside. Those buffalo robes kept out lots of cold.

*Mandan village, as painted from life by George Catlin.*
*Image courtesy of North Dakota State Historical Society*

# THE SOUTHEAST

*I.   Fargo – West Fargo – Valley City -- Scenic Drives – Jamestown*

*II.  Linton – Long Lake – Wishek – Ashley – Fort Ransom – Rutland*

This section presents two options for seeing southeast North Dakota, one starting in Fargo and heading west, the other coming east from Bismarck. Feel free to drive in reverse order if that's your choice.

Geography looms large around here. Natural lakes, wide rivers and their valleys, and more hills than you might imagine give this region dollops of scenery and much traveler appeal. While fishing and hunting have always been and will probably always remain the most common ways folks connect with the outdoors in North Dakota, there's increasing interest in birding, hiking, bicycling, kayaking and other activities that require no license or camo.

Really good news: **there is only one area code for the entire state of North Dakota**. That's why, here and throughout this book, phone numbers are given without those three initial digits. Wherever you go, it'll be 701.

## FARGO

Because Fargo is North Dakota's largest city and maintains its biggest airport, many travelers begin their journeys here.

It helps if you like trains. Fargo has always been joined at the hip to the railway lines; one of its principal streets is named NP Avenue, for the Northern Pacific line that for many years was the only route from civilization, i.e. Minneapolis, into the Dakota frontier. Today the tracks still run through downtown, and one of the first sounds many folks hear as they exit the airport is the big-band blart of a train horn.

As to Fargo culture: first of all, there's that movie. For too many people across the country, if the question is "Fargo," the answer is always "woodchipper." Sure, Joel and Ethan Coen made one ripper, so to speak, of a good film, but they're on the record as saying, "The only reason we named it 'Fargo' is because that sounded better than 'Brainerd,'" a small city in their native Minnesota. For reasons known only to them, the Fargo city fathers have let the mischaracterization

11

remain and even abetted it, giving the woodchipper prop from the movie pride of place in the Chamber of Commerce

Forget the movie. Downtown Fargo is hip, young, party-minded but still small enough for a good walking experience. This is a city where cars still park on the diagonal (actually, it's like that all over the state. Not kidding). Leafy residential streets end in riverfront cul-de-sacs. Shoppers come from all over the state for retail binges in the malls and boutiques. Locally-owned coffeeshops, small vibrant theatres, independent bookstores and sleek Eurostyle design emporia share the streets with pancake houses, mom & pop diners, and an old-fashioned storefront radio station where passersby can look in and see announcers speaking on the air in real time.

*Storefront radio station, Fargo*

The city's tallest building is also the state's tallest. That would be the **Radisson Hotel** (201 Fifth Street North, 232-7363). Despite its size (fifteen stories) and its impressive, brightly-lit, portiere-style entrance, the hotel actually occupies only about a third of the building, the rest given over to investment and law firms. The lobby is smallish, but its bar is always humming. There's a restaurant on the second floor with typical (read: overpriced) hotel food, and a fitness complex on the same level with whirlpool, exercise room and the unexpected pleasure of a steambath. No swimming pool, though: the Jacuzzi and steambath occupy two corners of a large tile room that looks as if there might have been a pool there, but there isn't. In a state where every offramp chain down to the Super-8s has a covered, indoor pool, this lack at the Radisson is inexplicable.

Rooms at the Radisson are large, with dark furnishings and wide windows. The traditional look makes the place seem somewhat dim, but management has wisely added LED spotlamps on flexible arms next to the beds, making bedtime reading a pleasure instead of an exercise in squinting. Closets are set off at an angle, making the room look bigger, but there is no closet door, only a flimsy curtain in front of the space. Why?

One of the joys of North Dakota, and Fargo in particular, is the overwhelming presence of free parking. You don't get that at the Radisson, but you do park in a city-owned garage connected to the hotel and costing only $3. per day. There's also a covered, overhead bridge between the hotel and the Convention Center, convenient for the many groups that hold meetings, seminars, exhibits, and so on at the facility.

When it's breakfast time, guests have a variety of choices other than $10 scrambled-egg plates at the hotel. Younger locals recommend the **Smiling Moose**, (2877 45th Street, 277-8800) a buzzy coffee hangout where morning fare is typically pastries and artisanal McMuffin-like sandwiches. For a sit-down meal, walk south across the tracks to the **Fry'n Pan Family Restaurant** (300 Main Avenue, 293-9952) praised in city forums as being "just like Denny's, only the food tastes good." Prices are right at the Fry'n Pan: two eggs, links or bacon and toast weigh in at only $4.99, and juice, potatoes, etc., will add only a couple of bucks to that price. Although anybody with a hangover might want to avoid looking at the red-orange carpet with its geometric swirls, this place is perfect for the traveler who wants an instant feel for North Dakotedness. Walls feature photos of downtown in former eras, and the clientele ranges from retirees to families to local businesspeople.

There are many interesting shopping spots in downtown Fargo, but a few stand out. **Frontier Americana** (114 Broadway, 241-4140) is a weapon fancier's dream, with patina-laden firearms ranging from pre-1800 flintlocks (who knew Ethan Allen made guns?) to WWII Mausers and Arisakas. There's much more here besides guns, though. Treasures on sale range from authentic Native American beaded bags to the "Naughty Nellie" boot jack, a molded nude female figure with red hair and a saucy stance, to the priceless "Seabury's Sanitary Pocket Cuspidor," an ingenious U.S. Army invention for discreet tobacco chewers. Anybody in the market for Western art, including bronzes and sculptures, should check Frontier Americana's sizable collection. They do appraisals, too, so here is the perfect place to find out if Grandpa's captured samurai sword or Grandma's butter churner is the real thing.

Warm woods and subtle colors distinguish **Scandesign** (110 N. Broadway, 365-0900), an airy, two-story furniture and accessories store in an exposed-brick setting. Designers reflect a Northern heritage, with names like Ekelund, Luonto, Jesper and Tvilum along with Georg Kovacs (lamps) and Replogle (globes). Forget that big-box blue-and-yellow place out on the interstate: this is furniture you don't assemble, and pressboard would be as out of place here as a marimba band. Scandesign is not a bargain house: a marked-down cabinet will still set you back over a thousand dollars. Quality, however, is never compromised, either here or in their Grand Forks branch.

That increasingly endangered species, the independent bookstore, flourishes in Fargo under the name of **Zandbroz** (420 Broadway, 239-4729). New titles, classics, kids' books and unexpected finds are cleanly laid out, in an uncluttered setting. They feature a huge selection of books on local topics, and maps going back to pioneer times. Although North Dakota State University is just blocks away, this isn't a student bookstore: romance, sci-fi and mystery fans will find plenty of well-stocked shelves. Zandroz is a perfect place for ducking into during rain (or snow) and wandering in search of cookbooks, poetry or Red River lore. Service is friendly and knowledgeable; books are seldom discounted here, but watch for sales.

When it's time for dinner, stroll down to the **HoDo Lounge**, part of the restored and historic Hotel Donaldson (101 Broadway, 478-6969). The restaurant is clubby and just a little edgy with its mosaic wall made of found objects; the food is thoroughly thought out, sophisticated, and locavore-friendly, with state-sourced beef and vegetables on hand. Despite some dishes having silly names like "Emperor Ryan's Forbidden Chicken" or "Green Freakin' Wheat Balls," prices are quite reasonable for what is, in most people's minds, the best place in downtown Fargo, and you'll be pushed to find an entrée over $20. The HoDo's downtown location makes for comfortable tippling, since if you are staying nearby you can walk – or stagger – homeward safely. Fargo's streets are wide, clean and graffiti-free, and even here, many residents don't lock their cars.

The **Fargo Theatre** (314 Broadway, 239-8385) is another downtown icon. Art Deco movie palace was originally built back in 1926, and since its 1999 restoration, it's been host to plays, concerts and special events throughout the year. They still show movies as well, but they do it the old-fashioned way, with a live organist performing before every show. Visitors love the acoustics and the comfortable seating. On the second floor, there's a wood-carved statue of actress Frances McDourmand in her role as – you guessed it – Police Det. Marge Gunderson in the movie that bears the theatre's name.

Straying back to high culture for just a moment, the **Plains Art Museum** (704 First Avenue North, 232-3821) makes for a few hours or a full day of prairie aesthetics. This is not a showcase for exclusively Western art: among the artists in their permanent collection are pop guru

James Rosenquist and Impressionist painter Mary Cassatt. The museum is also home to some thought-provoking contemporary art by Star Swallowing Bull, Frank Big Bear Jr. and Luis Jimenez, along with lifetime learning opportunities and education programs. Admission is always free to members; non-member adults pay $5., except on the second and fourth Thursday of the month, when everybody gets in free.

Speaking of art, Fargo travelers often notice the colorfully-painted buffalo that cluster around popular street corners. This is a reminder that the state's second largest university, **North Dakota State University**, is located just north of downtown Fargo. Their teams, the Bisons (pronounced Bi-zons) often play in the **Fargodome** (1800 North University Drive, 241-9100), a weatherproof facility that hosts entertainers such as Pink and Justin Timberlake when it's not filled with green-and-gold-clad Bison fans. NDSU is a full-accredited land grant university that offers graduate programs in engineering, education, IT and other fields in addition to a complete undergraduate arts and sciences curriculum. The number of bars in downtown Fargo testifies to the student presence, but things are rarely out of hand and there is none of the town-gown conflict found in other college towns. The university's **Germans-From-Russia collection** (North Dakota State University Library, 12th Avenue North and Albrecht Boulevard, 701-2316) contains papers, artifacts and other evidence of North Dakota's second-largest ethnic group.

For everything you can't get downtown, there's the familiar shopping strip just south of town. Here all the household names from Best Buy to Wal-Mart cluster together next to fast-food and chain restaurants and Inns of various persuasions. Sure, it's all a little tawdry, but if you absolutely, positively have to have an HDMI cable, say, or a phone charger to replace the one you left at home, you'll find yourself pulling into one of these capacious parking lots sooner or later. At the **West Acres Mall** (3902 13th Avenue South), shoppers will find all their favorite stores along with the **Roger Maris Museum**, an accessible collection of photos and memorabilia commemorating the career of the great New York Yankees outfielder who hit 61 home runs -- back in 1961, before steroids were invented. Maris, a Fargo native and apparently a modest guy, insisted that, if he had to have a museum, "put it where anyone can see it and don't charge for it." Done!

The strip extends into adjacent West Fargo which is, conveniently, where we will find our next stop.

## BONANZAVILLE

North Dakota, like other plains states, has its share of heritage parks, a name coined for a place where you wander among pioneer artifacts. If you have time to visit just one of these, **Bonanzaville** in West Fargo is an outstanding choice. What's here are period buildings, furnished and grouped to represent a typical small town of pioneer times, as well as airplane hangars and similar buildings full of unexpected treasures.

How unexpected? How about a steam locomotive at least two stories high, bearing a mean, wicked wedge of a snowplow the size of a garage? There are all matter of trains here, as well as cars, horse drawn and steam-powered vehicles, and farm equipment to bug the eyes of any traveler with a pulse. And that's far from all.

There are 43 buildings here to explore, and almost half a million artifacts. The entry charge is $10 for adults, perhaps the greatest time-travel bargain in the state. (*Bonanzaville, 1351 West Main Ave., West Fargo, (282-2822, May through September).*

### Pioneer Village

North Dakotans like moving things. In fact, they seem to have a predilection for moving large objects, such as houses, churches, or entire towns, from one place to another, usually for practical reasons such as avoiding floods or being closer to a railroad. On this grassy, gravel-paved stretch of Bonanzaville, eleven vintage structures have somehow migrated here from other parts of the state. You'll see an authentic blacksmith shop, a one-room school, a meeting hall, a furniture store, and several cabins. There's a complete theatre ready for performances. Some buildings such as the creamery are replications, and in a few cases the contents of a home or business have been moved here intact. That would include the medical and dental displays, and the drug store.

Don't miss the **Embden Depot and Train Shed**, from 1900, which houses trains and parts of trains from 1883 through 1930. That's where you'll see the locomotive, passenger car and caboose. That gigantic snow plow reminds visitors of what it's like in North Dakota six or seven (some say eight) months of the year.

The following Bonanzaville attractions are all considered part of Pioneer Village.

### Moum Agriculture Museum

Prepare to be impressed by this array of food-growing apparatus from the 1880s until now. John Deere invented the molded steel plow in 1837. Horses, mules or oxen pulled the plows that broke the plain. In the early

20th century, motorized vehicles chugged their way onto the farm, and the rounded radiators, toylike steering wheels, and snug seats of these early models began to take on recognizable forms.

Travelers seemingly can't get tired of all the ways farmers were, and are, constantly tinkering with ways to kill weeds, dump chaff, seed, feed, water and protect their crops with a minimum of labor and a maximum of safety and efficiency (see **"A Field Guide to Farm Equipment"**). One trend is obvious: as farms got bigger, so did the machines. Go ahead – climb up into the cabs. Feast your eyes on switches, buttons, dials and gear shifters, and try to imagine tearing up the back 40. It's a kid's dream come true, whatever age you are.

*They wouldn't let me drive it home.*

### Dahl Car Museum

Even if you don't know a Studebaker from a Thunderbird, you'll enjoy this capacious space filled with internal-combustion-driven hardware from the past hundred years. Drool over the collection of '57 Chevys, candy-colored classics from the Era of Big Fins. Run your hand over the sleek curves of 1930s Packards and 1940s Plymouths, and blast off with the rocket-inspired design of the '50 Ford. This museum concentrates on American cars, which is just fine considering where it is; North Dakota youth were never big on Lamborghinis, anyway. You may emerge, as we did, wondering why cars aren't *colorful* today. Must a car look like a kitchen appliance?

### Horse-Drawn Vehicle Building

Everyone knows what a stagecoach is, but when was the last time you saw one up close? This is the place to contemplate a Western road trip, 1840s-style. Covered or Conestoga wagons abound (someone has called them "the first Winnebagos"), along with still-shiny red fire engines, gigs, buggies, farm wagons, and much more. Visitors with a taste for the macabre can imagine themselves, or the victim of their choice, making a final journey in the filigreed black hearse donated by a local funeral home. Before cars, people didn't just sit at home; they harnessed Old Dobbin, got out and did things, just as we do today. It's good to remember that sometimes.

### Telephone Pioneers of America Museum

How do you know when you're getting old? When you see your own possessions in a glass museum case. That's what happened to this author, when she glimpsed her baby-blue dial phone, *circa* 1973, in this fascinating place along with heavy, heavy black phones from the 40s and wooden wall models from Ma Bell's earliest days.

The museum takes up two distinct rooms, and visitors in one can call their families and friends in the other. Listen to the clicking of mechanical relays and understand that the telephone system of the 20th century was the *ne plus ultra* of electrical, as opposed to electronic systems. Here was a technology utilized by every person over five years old, as ubiquitous then as wireless today but, on the face of it at least, far less complicated. Have someone call you from the other room, see and hear the relays clicking, and feel the vibration of the actual bell on the first ring. While you're there, don't miss the unusual shapes telephones have taken over the years, including the pink Princess phone and a chunkier brown model apparently meant to represent a football.

There's also a large space given over to an old-style telephone switchboard, reminding guests that, once upon a time, every phone call was answered by a real, live person.

## VALLEY CITY – SHEYENNE SCENIC BYWAY – FORT RANSOM

This book defines the southeast as east of N.D. Route 3 to the Minnesota line, and south from U.S.52/N.D. 200 to the South Dakota line.

I-29 runs south from Fargo, paralleling the Red River, while from east-west I-10 turnoffs head north to Mayville, Cooperstown and Carrington, and south to Wishek, Ellendale and smaller towns.

This area is flattest by the river, but rolls and twists in some remarkable ways through Sargent, Ransom and Barnes counties. Here, as in its northern counterpart next to the Canadian border, hardwood forests cluster along draws and streams, their rounded, uniform green tops looking like a Grant Wood painting. In fall, the foliage rivals New

England's. Lakes are ever-present here, as the prairie pothole region, a geological formation and a glaciation remnant, begins in Sargent County and stretches all the way to Saskatchewan (*see* **Geography**). National grasslands, scenic routes, a fish hatchery and wildlife refuges make southeastern North Dakota a real draw for outdoors types, but it is agriculture in a major key that sets the tune. Locals take genuine pride in their towns, and it's still not unusual to find farms held by the same family for three or four generations.

## VALLEY CITY

Only sixty miles from Fargo on reliable, seldom-crowded I-94, Valley City occupies a unique place in North Dakota topography. Where ancient Lake Agassiz once lay, the Red River Valley contains the lowest point in the state (750 feet above sea level). Starting west of Fargo, the Drift Prairie begins to roll in gentle hills toward the Missouri Escarpment, a plateau that rises west of the Missouri River. Finally, the prairie pothole region, a vast swath of glacier-carved lakes and wildlife-friendly wetlands, tears right through here in its northwestward path. Valley City is the place where these three distinct land types come together, resulting in some of the most attractive natural areas in the state.

With a state university, a pedestrian-oriented downtown, and the state's only officially registered waterfall, Valley City is a great place to savor North Dakota's variety.

Let's hope you fulfilled all your big-box shopping needs in West Fargo, because Valley City (population 6585) is mostly chain-free. There are Leevers and Marketplace grocery stores plus a smattering of antiques dealers, bookstores, quilting shops, art galleries and other sellers of supposed nonessentials.

**Dutton's Parlour** (256 Central Avenue North, 845-3390) is the local go-to place for coffee and ice cream, while **Another Time** (106 5th Avenue Southwest, 845-3171), housed in a converted old-time house, draws praise for its fresh ingredients, friendly service and homemade pies, and has recently begun serving Mexican specialties. Always open for breakfast and lunch, it's wise to call ahead if you want dinner.

## SHEYENNE SCENIC BYWAY (Baldhill Dam-Lisbon)

These sixty-three miles of winding pavement, punctuated by interpretive signs, feature stands of hardwood trees, railroad history and at least one picturesque bridge on the way to **Fort Ransom**. Acclaimed by *Midwest* magazine as a prime viewing source for fall color, the Byway is a four-season destination, with Nordic and Alpine skiing, snowshoeing and snowmobiling in winter, followed by fragrant and evocative lilacs in the spring. Behind Baldhill Dam at the north end of the Byway, **Lake Ashtabula** beckons watersports aficionados with summertime boating, waterskiing and personal watercraft play.

Below the dam, the **Valley City State Fish Hatchery** harbors walleye, pike and perch. If you've never been to a fish hatchery, this place has your name on it. Kids and adults love to see the piscine inhabitants in their various stages from fingerling to full-sized, and there's a shady pond for catch-and-release. Picnic tables and walking trails help make the hatchery a destination. It's free, too.

## FORT RANSOM

South of I-94, the Sheyenne River Valley Byway goes by many names, all of them confusing. Heed the Scenic Byway signs, stay on the road that hugs the river, and you should be all right.

Fort Ransom: it's a fort, it's a town, it's a state park, and it's all in the county of the same name, honoring a brevet Major General and Civil War hero named Thomas E.G. Ransom. **Fort Ransom State Park** (5981 Walt Hjelle Parkway, 973-4331) is a much-prized playground and heritage repository. Among its attractions are two homes built by early settlers from Scandinavia, the Bjone/Olson House and the Sunne Homestead. These gutsy families were among the first to venture into the area back in the 1880s.

The park pays tribute to these and other hardy souls twice a year, during **Sodbuster Days** (second full weekend in July, first weekend after Labor Day). Period costumes, machinery and horse-drawn vehicles will be on hand, the point being to present a nineteenth-century homestead scene just as it existed in its own time. Here's your chance to watch and hopefully learn the arts of flintknapping, spinning, paper-cutting and, of course, watermelon seed-spitting (yes, there is a contest). The Days present plains farmers at a particularly interesting point in their history: mechanization was just under way and agriculture would never be the same again.

Fort Ransom State Park also offers camping, fishing, and canoe or kayak rentals in season. There are no horses available to rent, but if you and your friends choose to bring your own mounts, two group campsites have been set aside for equestrians. Facilities are of the outhouse persuasion, and admission is $5.

**Fort Ransom-the-fort, three miles south of the park,** got its start in 1867, nine years before the Battle of the Little Bighorn, at a time when the Plains Indians began to realize that their food supply and way of life were in serious danger of extinction thanks to their ever-increasing white neighbors. Although no intact buildings remain today, and in fact the fort itself only lasted five years (it was dismantled to build another fort), it's instructive to see the site and understand the soldiers' isolation in what was then a wilderness. Water had to be hauled 900 feet from the nearest spring, and roads in and out of the fort were frequently impassible due to snow, mud and flooding.

With a population of 77, the **town of Fort Ransom** won't suit the seekers of bright lights, but it does put on the Sheyenne Valley Arts & Crafts Association's annual show and sale, usually held on the last weekend in September. For a nominal fee of $2, visitors can watch craft demonstrations ranging from hair beading to glassblowing. Then it's time to chow down on pie and coffee, Scandinavian meatballs, and a turkey barbecue, and take in entertainment ranging from rock and roll to folk and sacred music.

Stay in a local B&B (there are several) or try a chain motel in Lisbon. From here, you may opt to continue south on Highway 32 to Route 11, which runs a little east to **Rutland**, or you may travel back to I-94 (via Highway 13 west to Highway 1 north) and continue to **Jamestown.**

## JAMESTOWN

Remember NP Avenue in Fargo? Jamestown is another place that owes its existence to the Northern Pacific. Founded in 1871, this is one of North Dakota's larger cities with approximately 16,000 people. You'll find a Walmart here, but the real draw has to do with a large, horned, furry quadruped in the cow family that once upon a time roamed the area in huge herds.

You guessed it: buffalo. Not only does Jamestown boast "Dakota Thunder," the world's largest buffalo monument made entirely of concrete, there is a real-life herd available for viewing year-round. By some miracle or via judicious breeding, that herd includes three authentic, born-that-way white buffalo. Native Americans considered white buffalo to be sacred animals, and Jamestown treats its own with reverence and the best in veterinary care.

While the Red and the Missouri are the state's major rivers, the James is no slouch either. Rising in the hills northwest of here around the town of Fessenden, the James curves to the southwest and then flows in almost a straight line, continuing through South Dakota until the Missouri gobbles it at Yankton. Along the way are lakes, streams, and recreation areas, with plenty of scope for birdwatchers as well as fishing folk.

## Dakota Thunder

Although he's been around since 1959, when he was created by local concrete sculptor Elmer Peterson, **Dakota Thunder** (404 Louis L'Amour Lane, 251-9145) only received his name in 2010. At twenty-six feet fall, D.T. is one imposing bison, and you've got to pray he stays upright: this animal weighs sixty tons. You can gawk at him all year, although hours differ in the fall and winter, and the gawking is free.

## Pioneer Village

If you missed Bonanzaville in Fargo, or if the experience just whetted your appetite, don't miss Jamestown's **Pioneer Village**, located at the same address and phone as Dakota Thunder, above. With a restored NP railroad depot, a gift shop, an art gallery and the writing shack of renowned Western fictioneer Louis L'Amour, you'll find plenty to see and do here. Costumed interpreters are on hand in the summer months to help explain things, and concessionaires offer pony rides for the kids and stagecoach sorties for everyone. Watch out for the occasional staged shoot-'em-up, and enjoy musical entertainment as well.

Pioneer Village closes for the season on October 7, and opens again on Memorial Day. Admission is always absolutely free of charge.

## Chan San San Scenic Byway (Adrian-LaMoure)

This historic and charming road begins south of Jamestown, where Highway 281 crosses Highway 46 just east of the James River. From Highway 46, take Route 63 south (you'll see signs). Here the tall-grass prairie waves and ripples alongside the winding river, and travelers on horseback can easily see themselves in the role of pioneer. If you should hear some warbled strains of "My Fair Lady" or "Fiddler on the Roof," you are not hallucinating: the **LaMoure County Summer Theatre** presents classic Broadway musicals throughout the summer.

There's also an officially listed **Historic Courthouse** in LaMoure, but perhaps the most offbeat attraction here is the one-of-a-kind **Toy Farmer Museum**, which is exactly what it sounds like. No plastic cows here: the museum, founded by lifelong hobbyists Clair and Cathy Scheibe, specializes in intricate if tiny reproductions of authentic farm equipment. Housed in a 1916 barn that was moved to its present occasion (there they go, moving buildings again!) in 1946, the museum was configured in 1992 and has been going strong ever since. The late Mr.

Scheibe and the still-with-us Mrs. Scheibe also publish several magazines geared to farm-collectors, headquartered in LaMoute (7496 106th Avenue SE, 883-5206).

From here, we suggest traveling east on rural Highway 13 to **Linton.** Alternatively, if you are coming west from Bismarck, take I-94 east to U.S. 83, then head south to the junction with 13 and go east.

## LINTON

At the other end of southeast North Dakota, on U.S. 83 sixty miles south of Bismarck, is peaceful Linton. Wide streets, white clapboard homes, churches on green, clipped lawns and centenarian buildings on Main Street: Linton is about as typical as a town of 1100 people is likely to be in this part of the state. Founded in 1907 and still the seat of Emmons County, Linton is home to an imposing **courthouse,** built in 1934 by FDR's Works Progress Administration: you could probably fit all the residents inside and still have room. Incidentally, the prior courthouse was a lean-to and an assortment of shacks dating back to 1901.

*Emmons County Courthouse, Linton – Art Deco on the prairie*

Just north of Linton on Highway 83, **Long Lake** will make you pause. This is another U.S. Fish and Game Department Wildlife Refuge, and those who drive the easy gravel road to the park headquarters will find fishing platforms, restrooms, and what seems like an endless ribbon of blue water. Canada geese, bald eagles, herons and cranes all pass through here, as do stunning white pelicans that fly in formation and peel off one by one like slow dive bombers. Got ducks? North Dakota does, from mergansers to mallards, and it's always a pleasure to see a mama duck leading her string of offspring, just like on the nature channel.

After this, chow down at **Webo's** (212 S. Broadway on the east side of town). On Sunday mornings after church, the whole town seems to gather here for hearty German-Russian specialties. *Knoephle*, or dumplings, pop up in soups and stews, while the cucumber salad (in sour cream sauce) wins friends from all over. Yes, they have pies with tender, flaky crusts, and there are other salads on the menu. Good old American-style coffee (sorry, no charred beans here) makes the meal memorable, even if you're sitting around one of the two U-shaped counters up front.

## WISHEK/ASHLEY

In Emmons County, the predominant ethnicity ceases to be Scandinavian and starts to become German-Russian (*see* **Germans from Russia***)*. This sizable group of North Dakotans, descended from ethnic Germans who lived in Russia before 1917, has its own traditions, foods and celebrations. Southwest of Jamestown, at the intersection of Route 281 and State Highway 13, the town of **Wishek** embodies the farm-and-family ethos of these erstwhile pioneers.

With one thousand people, more or less, Wishek maintains the usual coterie of stores plus some unusual offerings: a 24-hour fitness center, for example, a municipal pool and a golf course. This is cattle ranching country for the most part, although corn, wheat and soybeans grow here as well. Because of its location on the North American flyway, Wishek is popular with hunters and birdwatchers, and at different times of the year local ranchers often rent out all or part of their property to those who hunt with rifles or binoculars. One of the most scenic sections of the prairie pothole region runs through here, with Green and Beaver Lakes being the closest to town.

One place to see in downtown Wishek is the **Case dealership**, home of farm-equipment-on-steroids (bright red this time). Notice the supersized tractors that have tank-style tracks instead of wheels; they are used for negotiating mud and wet conditions, common in the spring and fall, when even four-wheel-drive tractors can get mired down (see *Farm Equipment Checklist*).

On the same block as the Case dealership is an empty lot that, once ago, had a very unusual story to tell. We think of Northern Europeans as typical North Dakota ancestors, but there was one group that came here in the 1880s that had a different point of origin, a different mindset and a different religion. No trace remains of Wishek's Jewish community today unless you count that vacant lot, where a Mr. Trupin once had his butcher shop. His daughter Sophie eventually wrote a book about her rural upbringing, and you can be sure that Jewish farmers had as hard a time of it as anybody else.

# NORTH DAKOTA DREAMERS:
## THE JEWS OF WISHEK/ASHLEY

In Poland and Russia before World War I, those who practiced the faith of David were not permitted to own land, much less farm. Armed, officially sanctioned riots known as pogroms broke Jewish heads and ruined Jewish businesses on a regular basis. Tired of the hatred, sick of being crowded into cities and towns, many Jews came to believe that a completely new start was the best choice for their families. Why not America, the *goldene medineh* (country of gold)? Here, they reasoned, they could achieve self-sufficiency on the land and enjoy fair treatment by their neighbors. European philanthropists such as Baron de Hirsch set up agencies and gave grants, and Jews began arriving here in the 1880s and 1890s.

Until recently, the conventional wisdom was that the isolated, inexperienced pioneers, battered by the winters and ground down by farm labor, couldn't make a go of homesteading and failed miserably on the land. However, Professor Tom Isern of NDSU suggests otherwise, indicating that these settlers sold out after proving up to pursue other and better opportunities, often in retail, and to obtain higher education for their children. Many moved to Fargo, Minneapolis, Seattle and other larger cities, while others stayed in Devils Lake where they were successful clothiers, car dealers, salespeople and so on.

**Ted Mann**, founder of the Mann theater chain that at one point owned Grauman's Chinese in Hollywood and had screens in most American malls, was a Jewish native of Wishek, and **Sophie Trupin**, the butcher's daughter, wrote a memoir called *Dakota Diaspora* that tells the story of these unlikely pioneers.

Then there was **David Berman**. Known as "Davie," Berman was a native of nearby Ashley. Small-town life did not suit Davie. As soon as possible, he made a beeline for Minneapolis, where he became one of the city's most prominent gangsters, bootleggers and extortionists. Eventually Berman wound up in Las Vegas, where with his equally criminal partner, the late Bugsy Siegel, he helped found the casino business in all its raunchy splendor. Unlike most of his pals, Davie Berman lived to an old age and died in Vegas, on an operating table. His daughter **Susan Berman** became a journalist and wrote a book, *Easy Street*, that sang like a canary about the Las Vegas mob. In 2000 Susan Berman, then 45 years old, was murdered execution-style in her Los Angeles canyon home. Draw your own conclusions.

Travel south of Wishek on State Route 3 to Route 11, then go east on 11 to miniscule **Ashley.** North of town on an unmarked but obvious road, a small but well-kept graveyard, the **Ashley Pioneer Jewish Cemetery**, keeps its faith among the corn and wheat fields. Although the Hebrew inscriptions on the tombstones are faded, you can read the names and dates in English, and share the sorrow of these people whose unquenchable thirst for freedom and respect brought them so far to so strange a place. If you go, follow our Jewish tradition and place a pebble on the monuments. (*see **The Jews of Devils Lake**).*

# RUTLAND *AND THE* COTEAU DE PRAIRIE

Small towns in North Dakota come by the bushel, and each one promises the visitor a unique facet of the state. If you must pick only one, however – and that could be a fate worse than death – this book recommends **Rutland**, in Sargent County. It's an out-of-the-way place, about eight miles from the South Dakota border, and getting there is a process.

First, take Highway 11 east out of Ashley. You'll jog north for a bit on Highway 1, then continue east on 11 to Highway 32 south of Forman. **Do not turn on Highway 32!** Instead, stay on 11 a few more miles before turning south again on a county road (Sargent County #10) that is shown but not identified on many maps. Trust us – it's worth it.

What makes Rutland special? For one thing, although it harbors only 180 people, it is a fully functioning town that is in no way derelict or abandoned. North Dakota's roads are littered with the decaying corpses of farmsteads and hamlets that, in pre-boom days, were left to the elements, but Rutland is not one of these. Leafy, neat and well-maintained, Rutland has paved streets, municipal water & sewer systems, a well-equipped volunteer fire department, a bar, a restaurant, a general store, a bank, a former railroad depot that's now a museum, and a post office, among other establishments. In former years, it had its own schools including a high school (the Rutland Rockets) and an amateur baseball team (the Rutland Roosters) that had a powerhouse reputation in North Dakota baseball from the beginning of the 20th Century up to the 1960's.

For another, Rutland is the kind of place where, hackneyed as it may sound, citizens really do pull together to help each other. It's the kind of town that hosts spaghetti supper benefits to help pay residents' medical costs, and where no one is a stranger for more than half an hour. While they are fighting to maintain their independence and their own distinct facilities such as the post office, Rutlandians aren't cut off from the world. Computers and high-speed internet access are everywhere, and citizens tend to stay on top of national and world events. The community even has its own internet web site, **www.RutlandND.com**. With a well-educated, proud and resourceful group of residents, Rutland embodies all the best virtues of small-town life.

Stop in at the **Rutland Café** (you don't need an address – the whole town is four blocks long and six blocks wide) for a meal and a chat.

When night falls, do what the locals do and head for The **Lariat Bar**, down the block from the café. While it presents a blank face to the world, the Lariat is lively inside. Wood-paneled walls and high ceilings echo to laughter and the clinking of glasses, and if the café is closed you can get a fine meal at the Lariat (the appetizer special is a treat). Locally brewed beers are always available along with the familiar brands, and there's a pool table for a friendly game if you are in the mood. The bar and back bar have been in use since the 1880's, and the large western mural on the north wall was painted by a native American artist back in 1953.

At **Doreen's Design & Gifts**, check out the sparkly earrings and other jewelry, and save some space in your bag for something by local artist **Kathy Brakke**. A one-woman art whirlwind, Kathy's colorful murals can be seen downtown during the annual Uff-Da Day, a Fall Festival with a Scandinavian theme, and her quilts are on display at The Rutland General Store. Kathy's husband, **Bill Anderson**, is a County Commissioner, City Attorney, and unofficial historian of all things Rutland. If you meet Bill, ask him to tell you about Christmas in his childhood, when his father ran the depot and there was plenty of joy in the world.

**Paul Anderson**, a recently retired manufacturing company manager and Bill's kid brother, is president of the North Dakota Grape and Wine Association. Yes – wine grapes do grow here – and if you think this is a joke, remember folks laughed at Oregon wines, now a multi-million dollar business, and at California wines before that. Paul and his associates are looking for a winemaker, and by the time this book is published, they may be selling North Dakota's latest agricultural export.

There is a small RV park in Rutland, but no hotel or motel lodgings. However, seven miles to the southeast, with a Havana ND address, is the **Coteau de Prairie Lodge (www.CDPLodge.com)**, an unexpected bolt of luxury lightning sitting in splendid isolation on the highest hill for miles around. Designed by local farmer **Joe Breker** and his family, the Lodge has soaring ceilings, windows that go on for days, beautiful wood construction, and enough room for a wedding, seminar, church retreat or the occasion of your choice. There are 12 rooms plus a dormitory space. The huge and stylish kitchen, right out of HGTV, is open to guests who can bring and cook their own food (there's also a commercial kitchen for those big events). Breakfasts are do-it-yourself, with freshly ground coffee beans always on hand. The rooms are all ensuite, have flat-screen TVs, and are wonderful for relaxing after driving the three miles of gravel that take you here. Call **Olivia Stenvold** (680-1175) Joe's daughter, for information and reservations. Prices are surprisingly reasonable for this level of aesthetics and service.

This book recommends asking Joe Breker for an agritour of his 5000-acre farm. You'll hang with Joe, his brother, his cousins, and his son-in-law Austin as they herd cattle (with trucks and ATVS), and tend crops. Joe knows the natural history of the Coteau (pronounced koh-TOE), a region of hills and woods that begins in northwest Iowa and reaches its culmination right here. He can show you the stone markers that divide the state from South Dakota, and can tell you their dimensions, when and how they were placed, and who's been to see them lately. He's a proponent of no-till farming and the use of cover crops, and he'll gladly explain how these eco-friendly techniques work. It's well worth the drive to this comparatively out-of-the-way place to get a close and personal view of how agriculture really works, and how these smart, up-to-date people manage their wheat, corn and soybeans, and their Black Angus cows.

Bird fanciers and other nature lovers will want to find the U. S. Fish & Wildlife's Tewaukon National Wildlife Refuge headquarters at Lake Tewaukon, 3 miles east of the Lodge, 10 miles southeast of Rutland. The Refuge owns and manages an expanse of wildlife habitat in 2 units that stretch from Lake Tewaukon at the east end to Silver Lake, 5 miles southwest of Rutland. This is a great place for observing all kinds of waterfowl, upland birds, songbirds and big game animals such as whitetail deer and the occasional moose.)The website address for the Tewaukon National Wildlife Refuge is *http://www.fws.gov/tewaukon*.

After this, you may want to return to Fargo (take State Route 11 or 13 to I-29 and head north) before taking on another region rich in surprises and beauty: the northeast.

*Farmer Joe Breker and the other kind of "black gold" found in North Dakota.*

# SPECIAL FEATURE: *FARM EQUIPMENT CHECKLIST*

*... like birdwatching, only your targets are bigger*

If you're from a city where the biggest vehicle is your neighbor's SUV, you may have lots of questions about the outsized mechanized contraptions you'll see chugging around North Dakota fields. Here are some of the more common species, along with guaranteed unscientific notes about their form and function.

**GUIDE TO PLUMAGE:**
Green with yellow accents:—John Deere
Royal blue:—New Holland
Bright crimson-red:—Case, a North Dakota company (formerly International Harvester)
Yellow:—Cat, or Caterpillar

*(all photos by Sylvia and Isadore Wendel, unless noted)*

### BACKHOE
The bucket and arm attach to the back of the tractor. The arm pivots from a center position. Good for debris removal, burying large dead animals (well, they have to go somewhere), pulling out stumps, or digging a BBQ pit in which to roast large dead animals. *Courtesy of Shutterstock.com*

## BALER

This is a box on two wheels that hitches up to a tractor. Its purpose is to gather hay – which is not a kind of plant but a generic term used for plant material that becomes animal fodder. Once the hay is baled, or shaped into those giant's jellyrolls you see perched on fields throughout the state, it can be easily accessed or stored for use in the following year. This machine has curtainlike strips behind the front bar, and a serrated circular blade at the hitch for separating bales. Hay, or to employ the technical term *forage,* goes in, gets shaped into bales, and comes plopping out the back door.

## CHISEL PLOW

This unfolds and gets attached to your tractor, either with a draw bar or a 3-point hitch. It digs up land in spring before planting. Chisel plows dig up whole fields and are therefore only used when no crops are present. These just tear up the land; they don't plant anything. Chisel plows are frowned on by proponents of no-till farming, but they are still widely used throughout the state.

## COMBINE (aka HARVESTER)

Two wheels front, four wheels back. Front attachment cuts the crops. Crops are then sucked into the machine. The arm swings out to dump the clean crop into a truck. The truck then takes it to a train, where it is shipped to ports. From there, our American grain goes all around the world, feeding millions of people. North Dakota, and its neighboring states, are a global food factory, something that well-meaning locavores don't always understand.

Field→combine→truck→grain elevator→train→mill→bakery
→many, many cookies.

© Can Stock Photo - csp17159860

## SEED DRILL

Another tractor attachment. This is used to drop seed in rows. Depending on the type of soil, it can dig several kinds of rows. As the drill moseys across a field, the auger dumps seed into holes cut by the drill. *Courtesy of Shutterstock.com*

## SKID STEER LOADER

Used to move heavy items such as bales around the farm. May use tracks (like tank treads) instead of wheels. Caged cab protects driver in case of rollovers. Not a bulldozer – doesn't move dirt around.

**Bobcat**, a local brand manufactured in Gwinner, ND, is the most common brand seen in these parts – so common, in fact, that passengers deplaning at Hector International in Fargo will find shiny new, bright-colored Bobcat models parked in the concourse. Unfortunately, they cannot be rented by travelers looking for an alternative to the usual four-door sedan.

**SPRAYER**

For inorganic farming. These machines are supersized, so big that a person under 5'5" tall can stand inside the wheel. The tank on top holds the chemicals that are then sprayed out by the attachment behind the back wheels. Get upwind of these!

**TELEHANDLER**

The long arm has forklift-like prongs on it and telescopes (hence the name). It can pick up items in front or in back of the vehicle. This is what you want for picking up large quantities of fencing, hay bales or other flat, heavy items. A very versatile device, the telehandler saves time and farmers' backs with fewer "oops!" moments.

## TRACTORS

Your basic farm workhorse. Available in a plethora of sizes and configurations, including monster models with up to twelve wheels. Common amenities today include air conditioning, CD player, and multiple outlets for smartphones, tablets and laptops. Tweeting from the tractor? It's happening right now.

# BONUS FEATURE:
## *TALKING TO THE DEERE MAN*
### *an interview with Edwin Olson*

*Edwin Olson is a sales representative at Langdon Implement in Langdon, ND, selling John Deere equipment. Under a portrait of the company's founder, dated 1837 – "He gave to the world the steel plow" -- Edwin graciously took time out of his day one October morning to chat with the author and answer some questions.*

*Q. Why do some tractors have so many wheels?*
A. They're used for tillage. The more wheels your tractor has, the more traction you have. The more traction you have, the more ground you can till at one time.

*Q. What's the gas mileage like on these machines?*
A. "Mileage" isn't exactly the word, since farmers measure their fuel consumption by the hour, not the mile. That said, the average tractor will get 25 gallons per hour on diesel fuel. Larger machines like balers will use more fuel, of course.

*Q. How does that work? You can't drive your combine to the gas station ...*
A. No, you can't. Most farmers store fuel on their property. Ten thousand gallons is considered appropriate fuel storage on an average-sized farm.

*Q. What are the main crops in northern North Dakota?*
A. The big three are wheat; canola; and soybeans. Canola is used for cooking oil, and soybeans go into everything. After these come sunflowers, also grown primarily for their oil, and corn. Improvements in corn hybridization make it possible for farmers to grow that crop farther north than ever before, so we've got some of that too. Sugar beets grow to the east of here, in the Red River Valley.

*Q. Let's say you're a bright-eyed young graduate of NDSU's ag program, and you want to start a farm. What will you need?*
A. Well, let's see. The absolute minimum would be a tractor; a driller,

36

for placing seeds; a tiller, to plow up the soil; and a harvesting combine. That could cost more than $1,000,000 altogether.

*Q. How about land? How much would you need to get started?*
A. These days, 5000 acres is just about the minimum if you expect to make a profit. Those homesteading grants—168 acres – were a joke a hundred years ago. You could never make a living on that small a farm.

*Q. How much crop could you harvest on 5000 acres, and what kind of money could you make?*
A. If all went well and you grew sixty bushels of wheat, say, to an acre, you could end up making six million dollars in a year. If all went well, that is.

*Q. Tractors and farm machines in general have evolved a lot in the last 100 years. What trends do you see in ag equipment in the future?*
A. Even now, you no longer have to steer your tractor – it does all that for you. In the future, expect much farm equipment to be completely driverless. You may still have to sit in the cab right now, but that won't last forever.

*Q. There's always been some romance to crop harvesting: farmers hiring crews who race from border to border, cutting wheat as fast as possible while the weather permits. Does that still happen today in North Dakota?*
A. Hiring outside crews is on the way out. Most farmers today have the combines and crew on hand, or they can hire local workers if they have to. The problem with hiring outside crews is they're expensive, they have to work very fast so there can be mistakes, and they're always under pressure to move on to the next job. It's just not economical good sense today.

# THE NORTHEAST

*I. Ronald Reagan Minuteman Missile Site*
*II. Grand Forks – Pembina – Rendezvous Region – Icelandic State Park*
*III. Grand Forks – East Grand Forks – Langdon – Turtle Mountain Scenic Byway – International Peace Garden – Bottineau – Devils Lake*

Think trees. Lots of trees. Hardwood deciduous trees, which seem to have wandered in from other parts of the country. Now, place the trees on close-set hills, add sweeping rivers, ferns and horsetails, and of course plenty of farmland, and you'll have some idea of this particularly pretty and nearly unvisited quadrant of North Dakota.

Here we present two routes and a side trip, and frankly recommend all of them. The **Ronald Reagan Minuteman Missile Site** in Cooperstown is another reminder of the large role North Dakota played in Cold War one-upmanship. **Pembina**, on the Canadian border, is a farm-service town that derives much of its income from Canadians and boasts an impressive state-funded museum. Other must-sees in the far northeast include **Tetrault Woods State Forest** and impressive **Pembina Gorge**, preferably in fall when the green and yellow cottonwoods are accented by bright red shrubs. The **Rendezvous Region Scenic Byway** offers green river valleys and impressive overlooks. Don't miss tradition-filled **Icelandic State Park** with its own natural wonder, the **Gunlagson Preserve**.

In the heart of this region lies **Devils Lake,** the state's largest natural lake, with Indian and pioneer history thick along its shores. Not far away, retired Cold War missiles hunker down on the ground and extend far beneath it.

When you head west, you'll want to take the **Turtle Mountain Scenic Byway**, a gentle roller coaster ride over the Turtle Mountains. On your way to the **International Peace Garden**, travelers will get to savor tidy small towns like **St. John** and **Walhalla**, and a string of emerald, forested lakes. Then there's **County Road 5** from **Rolla** to **Bottineau** and beyond, which clamors for visitors' attention with some bustling towns and some, ah, unusual public sculptures.

Minus the badlands and buttes of the west, undisturbed by the fracking boom, the terrain here ranges from black fertile soil on the banks of the Red River to glacier-carved potholes to gently rolling hills to dancefloor-flat prairie. Around here, and all along the Red River Valley corridor that stretches to the Canadian border, farmers grow the Big Three – wheat, corn and soybeans – along with canola, sunflowers, and a few others not generally seen in the rest of the state, such as potatoes, sugar beets and edible beans ("edible", in this context, is farm-speak for pintos, navys and similar beans – not string beans!)

## Ronald Reagan Minuteman Missile Site

Going north from Fargo, one option on your way to Grand Forks is to angle west on Highway 200 off I-29 (take the Mayville exit) to the **Ronald Reagan Minuteman Missile Site** (555 113-1/2 Avenue NE Highway 45, 797-3691). This is one of only two places in the entire United States that provide public access to these black-nosed dealers of death, which fortunately for us all never had to be used. At this site, travelers first view exhibits detailing the history of the program as well as the idea of "mutually insured destruction" – in other words, had the USSR heaved nuclear missiles our way during the Cold War, these Minutemen in North Dakota and southern Arizona would have been launched automatically, reducing the aggressors to rubble within seconds of our own mass death.

Ponder that, while descending into the deep, vertical troughs and accompanying levels that house the missile itself (not to worry, it's a dud). Down here, contemplate the dial phones, big black knobs and wall-sized computers that controlled the fate of the planet during that decades-long game of chicken. You'll hear realistic sound effects as you imagine what it might have been like, sitting several hundred feet underground and wondering if you might ever have to make a call on that red phone.

It's a hideous prospect, and perhaps it's fitting that this site bears the name of the President many feel was most responsible for the Soviet Union's eventual demise. At any rate, admission is free, and the site is open seven days a week in the summer, three days a week from September to November, and by appointment only from 11/15 through 5/15 each year. Return on Highway 200 to I-29, and continue north.

## Grand Forks

At the south end of the northeast, thirty miles north of State Route 200, the third largest city in the state, **Grand Forks**, is also the home of the elite University of North Dakota (*see "The Fighting Who?"*), where future doctors, lawyers, entrepreneurs and other professionals get their training.

With around 52,000 people, Grand Forks is a medium-sized burg that's dominated by the red brick, classically styled campus buildings. All is sweetness and light in downtown Grand Forks, where small independent businesses serve the students and community, but this nest of charm isn't all there is. Just south and west of town stretches a big-box paradise that is low on aesthetics but can be important to travelers who need a Walmart, Petco, Walgreen's or just about any other well-known retail emporium. The strip allows downtown businesses to maintain its pedestrian-friendly mixture of restaurants, bars and stores in the face of what might otherwise be fatal competition. There are also a few relevant business in East Grand Forks, on the other side of the river in Minnesota.

### University of North Dakota

This is North Dakota's home for those who want to pursue a traditional arts-and-sciences education. English, foreign languages, history and the social sciences all maintain departments here, while many students opt for the outstanding math, chemistry and engineering programs. UND also features the state's only medical and dental schools and a law school (one highlight of campus life is the annual Malpractice Bowl, a football game between med and law students). Green, with wide lawns and well-tended flower beds, UND is a walking campus. For visitors, this is a good time to get out of your cars and ask the way to English Coulee, a murmuring stream which winds through the campus and city. Stretch your legs on the riverside walking and bicycling trails, or get into a conversation with UND students.

# ** THE FIGHTING ... WHO? **

They used to be the "Fighting Sioux." For many years the UND sports logo was a handsome Indian in profile, with picturesquely disheveled hair, a feather dragging at the back of his head, and a determined expression. Rendered in UND forest green and white, the Fighter suggested self-confidence and an overpowering will to win, qualities much valued by the actual Sioux now living in North Dakota, who adopted the logo and championed it.

That wasn't enough for the P.C. police. After years of legal entanglements, the U. was forced to abandon the warrior. "Fighting Sioux" gear was still available as of 2013, on the internet and in local stores, but supply may be limited.

The Indian head seems to have gone the way of the Indian who once graced nickels. There is no word on a new mascot or logo.

*The officially discontinued logo, as seen on a friend's jacket.*

**Festivals**

Grand Forks prides itself on hosting festivals that take place throughout summer and fall. The **Wine and Art Walk Week** guides visitors through local artists' studios, while keeping them well supplied with *vin* local and imported. The **Blues on the Red Music Fest** has been happening every year for four years now, bringing top guitarmeisters and harp players here to bang out twelve-bars by the hour. The **Empire Arts Center** provides an intimate venue for classical, folk and jazz performances. There's a **Family Fun Night** in July, when even little kids get to stay out late, and a **Tour the Trails Bike Rally** later in the year. You can get complete information about these events and more from **visitgrandforks.org**.

**Eat, Drink, Sleep**

For the big splurge, travelers recommend **Sander's 1907** (22 S. 3rd Street, (701) 746-8970). This is the place you take your kid when he or she graduates from the medical school – and, hopefully, already has the job to pay for it. With entrees between $28 and $40, Sander's is a departure from most places in North Dakota, but the food is universally acclaimed. Eurofood lovers will drool for the Roast Caraway Duck, done in typical Czech style and accompanied by kraut and dumplings. If you haven't caught walleye on your trip, try it out here, sautéed and bathing in *beurre blanc* . Sanders, not surprisingly, has a terrific wine list, but what does surprise is their carefully chosen collection of dessert and port wines, a nice touch not often seen even in larger cities.

If you're on a student budget, however, you'll probably opt for the **Toasted Frog**, 124 N 3rd St, (701) 772-3764; also in Bismarck). Brick-walled, high-energy and informal, the Frog makes and serves top-notch martinis, plus plenty of wine and beer. The chef, Scott Franz, is a native of the state, and he is dedicated to the use of fresh ingredients and healthful cooking methods, with many options for vegetarians and the gluten-allergic. This is not a hairshirt restaurant, however: grilled pork tenderloin and other hearty meats are on the menu, along with lavosh wraps, wood-fired pizzas, huge salads, and desserts.

As far as **hotels** in Grand Forks go, here's the bad news: they're all chains. There's no fixed-up, old-timey place like the Hotel Donaldson in Fargo. That being said, every chain you've ever heard of and plenty you have not is present, either in downtown (or very close to it), or along the shopping strip to the south and west. Given that there is a certain sameness to all those Inns and Suites (nobody uses the word "motel" anymore, as you may have noticed), you're best off checking with locals, visiting TripAdvisor or Yelp, or playing roulette on a hotel-bidding site.

**Across the River**

You can park in North Dakota and walk across the bridge to Minnesota. Almost immediately on your right, you'll find **Cabela's**, the mega-outfitter that draws hunters, fishermen and outdoor types the way bright lights lure moths. If you are unfamiliar with this culture, it can be breathtaking to land on this camouflage planet with its walls of firearms, not to mention the counters stocked with gleaming knives and fine collections of antique weaponry. Don't be scared: all guns and knives get checked on the way in and besides, a curious tourist always keeps an open mind. The biggest draw at Cabela's is their carefully built dioramas with lunging bears, skittish deer and growling cougars in replications of wild settings. You can also buy cute décor for your cabin, or warm socks, or knit caps, none of which have been known to endanger any species. Aisles of flies and lures tempt fisherfolk (if you're squeamish, think catch and release.) Everybody finds something they want at Cabela's.

Right across the street, and on the river, check out **Whitey's Wonder Bar** (121 Demers Ave, East Grand Forks MN, (218) 773-1831) for lunch, coffee or a drink. The bar itself is the wonder here: dating back to the 1930s, it's a curving marvel of steel and glass block, and other Art Deco touches abound. The menu features a local favorite, **beer cheese soup**, which combines two of the northern prairie's basic food groups in one hot, creamy bowl, and comes with popcorn, not crackers. The coffee's good, too, and in fine weather you can sit out on the patio and grok the Red River.

## PEMBINA AND VICINITY

The easiest way to get here is on I-29, a straight shot north from Grand Forks. **Pembina** (pronounced PEM-bih-nah), a town of roughly 600 people, is proud of its "firsts," and rightly so, as this place accurately claims to have been the first settlement in the Dakota territories (*see* **History**). Pembinans were also the first people to link trade between the Mississippi, at Minneapolis/St. Paul, and the Canadian prairie, specifically the Hudson Bay Company at Manitoba. Pembina is also the nexus of two lesser-known ethnic communities, the Icelanders and the Metis.

Here, around 1800, the first non-Indian child was born in the state. Those who live for irony will want to know that this little girl was black, the daughter of an African-American who worked for Alexander Henry, Jr., of the North West Company. While we're on the subject, the first so-called "white" child in the state was born here in 1807 to a worker at the post. The worker, known as "the Orkney Lad," had been dressing and working as a man for some time, but was sent back to the Orkney Islands with her child when she turned out to be a lass.

On its push towards Hudson Bay, the sizable Red River flows right past Pembina, and it was this watery highway that brought early settlers and that carried trade back and forth before the coming of the railroad. Most of us have only seen the Red on television, when it flooded the entire region in the nineties, but like Grand Forks and Fargo to the south, Pembina has dried out, rebuilt, and renewed itself with considerable vigor.

Animals, and I don't just mean the barnyard kind, have been important in the development and history of the Pembina area. A buck-toothed rodent whose skins made very fashionable hats brought French and English trappers here from eastern Canada as far back as the 1790s. When the beaver was gone, oxen loomed large. Gelded steers, which is to say castrated bulls four years old or older, were favorites of the pioneers for many reasons. Oxen were strong, easy to train, mostly docile, and in a pinch they could be sacrificed for food, although for most families this was a last resort. Oxen pulled covered or Conestoga wagons through mud and snow and over icy or flooded ground. Since they lived off the prairie they ate for free, which must have really endeared them to penniless immigrants.

While the Norwegians and the German-Russians are North Dakota's best-known ethnic groups, arrivals from Iceland swelled the local population in the northeast. Products of a small, volcanic island with little arable soil and frequent ash flows, the Icelanders became increasingly disgruntled with their Danish rulers and began to migrate in the 1870s. They soon adapted easily to North Dakota, despite the hot summers and the mosquitoes. In 1893, they dedicated the delightfully named **Thingvalla Lutheran Church** in nearby Mountain, and that church stood for 110 years until unfortunately destroyed by fire in 2003. Today the church site and its accompanying cemetery are a landscaped **Memorial Site**, organized and developed by the descendants of those early settlers.

**Metis** sprang up around the same time as the fur traders, hardly surprising since most of them were fathered by traders who enjoyed relationships with Indian women. The word "metis" means "mixed" in French, but rather than straddle two cultures the Metis forged their own identity. They spoke a mixture of French and Cree, adopted Catholicism as their religion, built ingenuous carts out of rawhide and wood, and in time took over the fur trade from Europeans. Meti women tanned hides, dyed them, and stitched them together to make clothing. They dried deer meat to make pemmican, the original Indian jerky that sustained many a traveler on the plains. As late as the 1880s, there were over 10,000 Metis living in or near Pembina, and they are still a vital force in the area.

Much of this history is on display at the **Pembina State Museum** (805 Highway 59, 825-6840), part of the State Historical Society. The museum's two well-stocked galleries feature artifacts going back to the Stone Age, highlighting contributions from natives and Europeans alike. What's especially remarkable here is the museum's observation tower. Standing a full seven stories tall, the tower soars above the landscape and provides 360-degree views of the farthest northeast you can go in North Dakota. The folks who work here are friendly and equipped with almost encyclopedic knowledge of their region and its history. The museum is free, but there's a $2 charge for the tower.

**Oxcart Trails**

In Drayton, at the southern edge of Pembina County just off Highway 29, there's a group dedicated to preserving the route and the experience of those Metis-designed ox carts, along with the rest of the area's rich heritage. Author Laraine Snelling, whose *Red River* novels chronicle the turbulent lives of an early Norwegian family, has offered workshops at the Oxcart Trails Historical Society, and enterprising members sometimes hitch up oxen to replica carts and head out along the trails that once ran from St. Paul to Winnipeg.

What made these carts unique was their home-built construction; no blacksmith would ever be needed to repair them, a huge benefit on the prairie where skilled ironworkers were thin on the ground. The Society also buys old buildings such as sod houses and wooden homes, moving them onto their site and restoring them to near-original condition. Contact the Society at 454-6103 to hear about their upcoming events.

*Repairing oxcarts, early 20th century*
*photo courtesy of Wikicommons*

## RENDEZVOUS REGION SCENIC BYWAY

This is an 11-mile stretch of gravel road that meanders through some of the state's most charming areas, including the Pembina Gorge. **Have a good local map** – not just a state map -- and be prepared to use it, as GPS can be iffy around here.

From Pembina, go south again on I-29 to Route 81 and turn west; this becomes State Highway 5 at the town of Hamilton. A few more miles take you to Cavalier, where the Byway begins.

The Rendezvous Region is home to the state's longest uninterrupted woodlands, and the undammed Pembina River forms the most extensive stretch of wild river in North Dakota. Don't rush, stop often, and wander where your feet (or your tires) may lead you. Believe it or not, there's almost no farmland along this road, which makes it even more atypical of North Dakota.

### Icelandic State Park

This is the best-known attraction in the Pembina area, and 100 campers per summer night can't be all wrong. Set in a rolling, wooded area with many cool streams and creeks, the best part of the park is a bequest from pioneer farmer G. B. Gunlagson who in 1963 donated 200 acres to form the **Gunlagson Nature Preserve**, the first of its kind in the state. This place is a dream site for birders and botanists. There are concentrations of rare species here in the lowland oak forest, where eastern, western and northern living things come together on the banks of the spring-fed Tongue River. Forests of horsetails and ferns give the feel of an ancient rain forest, and it is always cool and moist here even in midsummer.

Those fond of more active pursuits have the rest of the park. **Lake Renwick** is the hub of water-based activities, with everything from simple swimming to canoe and kayak rentals and a single boat ramp. In the winter, snowshoeing, cross-country skiing and snowmobiling take over. Campsites have electric hookups and a sewage dump. There are even three cabins for the tent-averse who still want to stay in this beautiful natural setting.

If you're on the Icelandic culture trail, don't miss the **Pioneer Heritage Center.** A striking white-and-black church joins other authentic, restored buildings that together present an accurate picture of life in the homestead days. Stop for a moment and picture yourself, alone with your family in this subtle wilderness of sky and land. That was pioneer reality, and those who endured it are all our ancestors, no matter where your own folks may have come from.

*NOTE:* As of 2013, the entrance to Icelandic State Park is reached via a detour. This involves some driving on gravel roads, but if all those RVs can do it, so can you. Engineers are retrofitting Renwick Dam, and the work is expected to be complete in 2014. Check conditions first at **http://www.parkrec.nd.gov/parks/construction_zone/construction.html**

## Gingras Trading Post

At Walhalla, turn north off the Byway onto Highway 32 to this State Historic Site. Metis entrepreneur Antoine Blanc Gingras was a big wheel in his day, eventually owning assets worth $60,000 (probably over a million today). Starting out as a fur trader, he built trading posts along the trail to Manitoba and hewed himself a store out of oak logs. It's still standing, one of the few authentic survivors of that long-ago time.

Volunteers have carefully painted the store in its original colors, based on still-visible scraps in the wood. This may be the only red-and-white, blue-walled, pink-ceilinged 1840s log structure anywhere in the United States; certainly it is the oldest building in the state. Visitors will want to read M. Gingras' story in the interpretive panels, and perhaps pick up some (reproduction) fur-trade tools in the store. Staffed by friendly, knowledgeable tour guides, the Gingras Trading Post offers a vivid look at an often-overlooked aspect of early life in North Dakota.

From here you can return to the Scenic Byway, or continue east on Highway 55 and contemplate the fact that, while you are not in Canada, you can see it from here; the distance to the border is less than five miles. Stay on this road if you'd like to head back into Pembina.

## Pembina Gorge

Some travelers claim that the **Pembina Gorge State Recreation Area**, located just west of fading Walhalla, is the most beautiful place in the state, and on the face of it they could be right. Unfortunately, parts of this lovely green location have been opened up to offroad vehicles, including trail bikes and 4-wheeled ATVs. You may wish to drive on and stop at the overlook (signed) and contemplate its classic, painterly beauty. Hikers, horse riders and mountain bikers are welcome to use the trails, while in summer it's possible to rent canoes and float down the serene river.

*Pembina Gorge*

# LANGDON

Travelers wanting to stay in northeast North Dakota have surprisingly few options. Pembina, Cavalier and Walhalla each have one or two motels and perhaps a B&B, although the latter are often located on unpaved roads with no sights or restaurants nearby. As a result, visitors tend to congregate in Langdon, a town of 2,000 or so. With a busy Main

Street along State Route 5, Langdon is a hub for area farmers. There's a John Deere dealership (see *Talking to the Deere Man)* grain elevators, seed cleaning and sales facilities, oil and tank dealerships and much more. As befits a central town, there's also a supermarket, drug store, lumber and home center, high school, movie theatre and hospital.

### Sleep

For many years Langdon had only one aging motel, but recently **Cobblestone Suites** has brought its apartment-style lodging to town, and the reaction is all positive. At Cobblestone, guests get a kitchen with full-sized refrigerator, stove and microwave. Basic utensils and flatware are included, as are flat-screen TVs with cable, free internet and parking.

Cobblestone serves a hot breakfast, and anyone who's stayed of late in a lodging chain knows the drill: eggs, sausage or bacon, potatoes, cereal, yogurt, pastry, juice and coffee, not to mention the omnipresent waffle baker with its little plastic cups full of goo, I mean batter.

There are a few head-scratchers to the hotel's design. The staircase between first and second floors is located outside of the building itself, and must be accessed with a key card. The staircase is enclosed against the elements, of course – this is North Dakota  and is well-lit and clean like the rest of the hotel, but still it's a little odd to have to go outside, as it were, when you just want some coffee in the lobby. Additionally, the meager exercise equipment shares its space with the laundry machines, which can make for a hot and humid environment, less than ideal for a workout.

### Eat & Drink

This part of North Dakota is more than a little rural, and with rural life there comes a different sensibility.

Not much has changed here in four or five decades, so you'll be doing some time-traveling. Especially in restaurants, what are givens in big cities may be altered or completely missing here. **Fresh fruits and vegetables are often hard to come by,** and so is spicy-hot food.

There is, however, an important distinction between unpretentious and unappetizing, and two restaurants in the Langdon area teeter dangerously close to that line, as far as this book is concerned.

To many people, the term "supper club" may connote sophistication, New York nightlife, glitz, glamour and champagne. *This is not what it means in North Dakota.* In places like Langdon, "dinner" is the midday meal, and "supper" is the meal you eat after 6 P.M. That is a semantic distinction, and not necessarily important, but when we noticed **The Stables**, a supper club just east of Langdon, we expected something not a little different from what we actually encountered there. Inexpensive chairs and folding tables are the order of the day. People arrive in their everyday working clothes. The salad bar did include lettuce, and a tasty broccoli-grape combination, but the other choices were all variations on the pasta or potato salad theme, and very heavy on the mayo. Cucumber salad, a local specialty, was caked with a thick sour cream dressing. As for side orders, the choices were baked potato; fries; sweet potato; and roasted baby potatoes.

If you are on a diet, this is emphatically not your place (but then, you should stay out of North Dakota). Beef was on the spongy side, although the roast chicken was well-done and tasty.

South of Langdon on State Route 1, follow the cars to the hamlet of Nekoma and a large wooden building on a gravel lot, labeled **The Pain Reliever**. This is an out-of-the-way place in an area that is already very much out of the way, but it is very popular with locals, and almost always crowded.

*The Pain Reliever, Nekoma*

What goes on at The Pain Reliever is something like a community potluck, only instead of bringing your own food, the restaurant cooks it for you. Covered dishes are placed on buffet tables covered in picnic-table cloths. Grab your plasticware, your paper plate and napkin and dig in (this is, of course, after you notify your server that you will take "the buffet.") There are veggie dishes as well as meats, and a salad bar much like the one at The Stables. This is as much a bar and social center as a restaurant, and all the patrons seem to know each other, and the servers, very well.

When you consider that your only other local choice is **Dairy Queen**, the two eateries mentioned here begin to make more sense. Of course, if you are staying at the Cobblestone, you have the option of visiting the local Leevers supermarket and cooking your own dinner, supper or what have you.

# THE GREAT PYRAMID OF NORTH DAKOTA

## OR HOW TO TURN SIX BILLION DOLLARS INTO
## HALF A MILLION DOLLARS

No, it isn't an outpost of Las Vegas, nor was it built by ancient Indians. The four-sided pyramid – and it is extremely large – that you can't help seeing on State Route 1, south of the intersection with State Route 17, is for real, and its existence is an interesting tale.

Back in the days of the Cold War, America worried a lot about Soviet missiles. Not without reason: those missiles got as close as Cuba at one point. The solution, of course, was to have our own missiles – but where?

Someplace where there isn't much else. Enter North Dakota, always in need of money and jobs pre-Bakken. They called it the Stanley R. Mickelson Safeguard Center, and its intent was to make sure no deadly Soviet ICBMs, or intercontinental ballistic missiles, reached this country. To this end, the government spent 6 billion dollars to build silos to house our own missiles, nicely tipped with thermonuclear warheads. The pyramid itself functioned as a missile control and radar system, intercepting signals from all points of the globe.

But not for very long. In fact, the facility was open for less than two years. Then it was shut down forever, because it cost too much and because, gee, maybe it's not such a great idea to detonate nuclear warheads over our own country. You think?

Today the paint on the buildings is rusting and the windows are starting to crack. Although still fenced with high barbed wire, the Great Pyramid complex is visible from a number of angles, and makes for great, spooky photography when the shadows are right. Also see *Ronald Reagan Minuteman Missile Site*.

*Update:* As of 2013, the entire facility had been sold to the Hutterites of Forbes, North Dakota, who would like to start colonies at the complex (see *Hutterites).* The Hutterites bought the Mickelson Safeguard Center at auction in late 2012, for $530,000.

*Not a joke. Not an optical illusion. The Great Pyramid of North Dakota.*

# TURTLE MOUNTAIN AND THE CHIPPEWA

Don't miss a chance to drive the **Turtle Mountain Scenic Byway**, a state-sanctioned stretch of Highway 43 between Rolla and Bottineau. This is a well-maintained paved road that plunges the traveler squarely into the middle of some of North Dakota's most attractive landscapes. With humped hills bumping each other, densely packed trees and the occasional long vista, it's something like a hobbit Appalachia, only an unpopulated one.

While summer does see vacationers plying the lakes and rivers in canoes, and winter brings out the snowmobilers and cross-country skiers, most of the time visitors will have the place to themselves. There are drawbacks to such isolation, however, in that the tiny towns along the route have limited dining, shopping and gas opportunities, and on Sundays, you can expect almost everything to be closed. Bring a picnic or a sack lunch.

Traveling the Turtle Mountain Byway requires some map-reading skills, since many roads are unmarked. From Bottineau, drive west on Highway 5 to Highway 14, then turn right (north). Look for Highway 43: there may be signs, or there may not. If you come to the Canadian border, you've gone too far.

Highway 43 is gravel in some spots, but passenger cars can get through without a problem most of the year. This is high, wide, isolated country, yet it is not a wilderness. Although there's seldom a soul to be seen, farm fields line both sides of the road.

In **Bottineau**, near the Byway's western end, history buffs will want to make a beeline for the **Four Chaplains Memorial**, one of several around the country commemorating the Catholic priest, the two Protestant ministers, and the Jewish rabbi who died together during World War II. Handing their life vests to others, the four linked arms and went down with their torpedoed ship. It's an inspirational story, and shouldn't be forgotten. Find the memorial in front of **St. Mark's Catholic Church** at 322 Sinclair Street. "Find" is the important word here, as the memorial can't be seen from the street: it's set back against the east-facing wall of the church, behind a pillar with a sundial, shaded by large trees. Sadly, the memorial is not well-known in town, and locals we met couldn't help us with directions.

Also in Bottineau, check out the **world's largest sculpted turtle**, riding the world's largest snowmobile (both made of fiberglass). "Tommy," as the turtle is affectionately called, resides in a park north of, and invisible from, Route 5. You'll have to leave the road and drive through town to find it, but fear not: everyone knows where the turtle is.

*Who says cold-blooded reptiles and snow don't mix?*

From Bottineau, jog north off the Byway to **Lake Metigoshe State Park**, a very large body of dammed water that looks somewhat blah after the smaller, more intriguing lakes between St. John and the Peace Garden. Still, the lake is popular for fishing competitions, and like Waterton Lake hundreds of miles to the west in Montana, it straddles the U.S.-Canadian border.

The Turtle Mountain area provides other familiar and offbeat attractions, ranging from a Stonehenge of sorts (**Mystical Horizons**, a series of steel and concrete pillars erected by a cosmic-minded engineer) to the **Dale and Martha Hawk Museum**, a repository of antique farm equipment, unique vehicles, and pioneer implements including pitchforks, threshers, and *lefse* (flatbread) rollers. Not to be outdone, Dunseith whacks your eyeballs with the **W'eel Turtle**, a 40-foot amphibian made entirely of tire rims, gathered lovingly by a local mechanic and welded together by artist Curt Halvorsen. This turtle's head had a motor and was movable, until humorless insurance people brought up the liability aspect. You may still climb on it, however.

Finally, put down the top and cruise on over to **Rolla** for the annual Ragtop Festival, where convertible cars of every size, shape and designation come together each year for parades, contests, games, a Fun Run and fireworks just before July 4th. Motorcycles, the original topless vehicles, are welcome too. Jump in nearby **Long Lake** to beat the heat. Hungry in Rolla? Try the **North 40 Café** (207 Main Avenue East, (701-477-0552), for a good burger and that seldom-seen miracle in these parts, a side salad with no added cheese.

Between Rolla and Belcourt on Highway 5 is the **Turtle Mountain**

**Reservation**, home to Chippewas and Metis and the inspiration for the unnamed "rez" in **Louise Erdrich's** terrific novels about North Dakota. In *The Round House*, she writes, "I know there's lots of world over and above Highway 5, but when you're driving on it … it seems you are balanced. Skimming along the rim of the universe." Exactly.

The Chippewa avoided open conflict with whites, preferring intermarriage and business partnerships with Europeans to the ways of war. Today, not surprisingly, much of their tribal income derives from the **Skydancer Casino**, in nearby Belcourt.

## INTERNATIONAL PEACE GARDENS

One place where you will see more than a few people is at the **International Peace Gardens** on the Canadian border, 44 miles north of Rugby on U.S. 281. This gardener's paradise was the brainchild of plant enthusiasts on sides of the border, who envisioned a beautiful place to mark the friendship between the U.S. and Canada. Workers from the CCC (Civilian Conservation Corps) built up most of the site in the 1930s, laying out gardens and shoveling paths. Today a nonprofit group administers the Peace Garden, and its laws explicitly state that half the board members be Canadian, and half American.

This is a vast, open park, beaming with pampered lawns and technicolor flower beds, including an outstanding rose garden. The gardens wind along paved paths lined with native trees from both nations. Kids may run free, but no dogs are allowed.

No one should leave the Peace Garden without seeing its latest addition, the **9/11 Memorial**. Even though you're standing over 1600 miles from Manhattan's Ground Zero, expect an eerie feeling on the back of your neck. Framed by the gentle forest, with a view to a lake beyond, the twisted steel girders lie burned and scarred, looking hot to the touch. The visual contrast, senseless death and living nature, will stir every sentient soul.

When the weather revolts, dive into the **Interpretive Center** and marvel at the **Conservatory**, where 6,000 species of succulents and cacti reside in climate-controlled comfort year-round. The gift of Minotian Don Vitko, these plants reflect a collection going back forty years and are not to be missed. Take a lunch break at the café and enjoy the gift shop before heading outside again to take in the **Sunken Garden** and the **Flower Clock**.

# PASSPORTS, EH?

The International Peace Garden straddles the border and you must go through Canadian Customs before entering the park. On your way out, expect to pass through U.S. Customs. The lines can be long in the summertime, so plan ahead. *U.S. citizens MUST show a valid passport at both checkpoints*. We don't want any more 9/11s. Visit **www.PeaceGarden.com** for the latest updates.

*On your left, Canada, On your right, the U.S.*

# DEVILS LAKE

From Langdon, head west on Highway 5 to Highway 20. Turn south on 20, proceed around 35 miles to **Devils Lake** and prepare to be fascinated. A perfect vortex of recreation, history, nature and all things unexpected, Devils Lake is worthy of a few days at least. Chasing ghosts? Check: there's a haunted post office. Chasing cash? Check: there's a casino for that. Shooting ducks for your dog to chase? Double check: this is one of the best waterfowl hunting areas in the state. Even non-hunters and those who go pale at the sight of a worm on a hook can thoroughly enjoy this congenial, scenic region.

**Devils Lake itself** spreads over Ramsey County like an outstretched hand, extending into Nelson and Eddy Counties and lying in a rough northwest-southeast axis. This is a no-outlet lake that collects runoff from the glacially-carved potholes, or round basins, that dot the area. It's hard to measure Devils Lake's surface area, as parts of it may dry up in drought years and increase again with heavy rainfall. Lakes like this are mostly shallow with a high salt content, but since the late 1990s, when 70,000 acres of farmland went under water thanks to spring floods, Devils Lake has been deeper and less saline than most.

Perhaps not surprisingly, controversy has erupted over the depth and content of the lake. After the floods of the 90s, the Army Corps of Engineers came up with a plan to build an emergency outlet for Devils Lake into the Sheyenne River. North Dakota's government, however, found the price tag too high, ignored the Feds, and built its own outlet, completed in 2005. That didn't satisfy Minnesota and the adjourning Canadian province of Manitoba. They combined forces and sued North Dakota, on the grounds that non-native and invasive species could somehow end up in the Red River and, eventually, Lake Winnipeg. That lawsuit fizzled when investigation showed there were no such invasive species present in Devils Lake.

Most visitors, however, will care less about such arcane goings-on and more about where they can launch their fishing boat. Devils Lake has good news for them: there are no less than 7 boat landings around the lake shores. Venture out on the water, and you'll discover **Graham Island**, a gem. Stop here and visit the state park which has reasonably priced cabins to rent for the night and picnic shelters for the day. There's even a meeting facility popular with local civic and church groups. Since fishing is king, expect to find an open bait shop in summer, along with those ever-fragrant fish-cleaning areas.

Also on the lake is the hilltop **Spirit Lake Casino**, run by the Sisseton Wahpeton Sioux. An eyesore or an oasis, depending on your point of view, the casino has Vegas-style gaming along with budget-friendly rooms and restaurants. Luxury suites, complete with Jacuzzis, welcome big spenders, and the parking lot is bigger than many towns elsewhere.

If casinos don't thrill you, ignore the bright lights and the ding-ding-DINGs, step away from the cigarette smoke and head instead for **Sullys Hill Game Preserve**, established by Theodore Roosevelt and meant to preserve bison and elk (admission $2, but well worth it). No guns or reels here; just an Interpretive Center, a scenic auto tour and lovely, shaded hiking trails included a self-guided one for identifying flora and, hopefully, fauna. Besides the two large quadrupeds beloved by T.R., look for ambulating fur coats belonging to foxes, mink, weasels and muskrats, along with brightly colored wood ducks (in season) and a variety of charming warblers. There's a prairie dog town, with a platform for viewing the cute little critters (they get nervous when you actually step on their turf). Like many areas in northeast North Dakota, this is almost an extension of the North Woods. Come in June for fireflies, and in July for wildflowers.

### DEVILS LAKE – The Town

The town of Devils Lake is good-sized by North Dakota standards, around 7000 people. There are a few chain hotels, several places to eat and some interesting, not to mention supernatural, sights. The red-brick downtown is intact, parallel parking is the rule and in any weather people are out taking care of their affairs. Or their appearance: Devils Lake boasts more than a few apparel stores, nails-and-hair shops, tanning salons, and a gym on Main Street where healthy folk are stepping and treading day and night. This makes sense when travelers understand that D.L. is where North Dakotans in six rural counties flock when they need almost anything they don't grow or make themselves.

Head straight for the **Old Post Office Museum** on 4th Street NE. This was an office building as well as a post office, and you can see the former offices of lawyers, doctors and (ouch) dentists. The major attraction, though, is the **Lillian Wineman Collection**, a treasure trove of fashion, furniture, jewelry and personal items dating from the turn of the 20th century and belonging to a prominent local woman (Wineman was connected to the Jewish community here. See *Sons of Jacob Cemetery*). Some folks, including museum employees, construction workers, and schoolchildren, swear they have had spectral experiences: footsteps on a stairway or corridor when no one is there, whistling in the ears, invisible hands gently pushing curious kids away from the late Lillian's possessions.

Skeptic, believer or somewhere in between, you should really check this out; just don't be surprised if a hundred-year-old hat lands on your head, for example, or an object turns up somewhere else from where you just saw it minutes ago. There have been many such unexplained phenomena, but never fear: the lady's spirit is said to be "meek and mild," and no wraith-seeker has been harmed to date.

## Old Main Street Café

This restaurant (416 4th St NE, 662-8814), much loved by locals, features the usual lunch items plus some Mexican specialties. The fajita sandwich comes on Texas toast, and chili can hit the spot on a rainy day. Service is friendly and prices are well within the reasonable level.

Across the lake to the southwest, the town of **Fort Totten** features its walled namesake. After a military post was no longer needed here, the Fort became an Indian boarding school. Whatever you may think about such establishments from today's perspective, this is where hundreds of Indian kids learned the English language and the 3 Rs. After a while, Fort Totten became a tuberculosis sanitarium and, finally, a grade school that functioned until 1959. The **Pioneer Daughters Museum** at the Fort features antique farm implements – yes, these are common in North Dakota, but it's instructive to see how food was grown before mechanization – and letters home from a 19th century soldier, written in his native German to his immigrant parents. Be aware that the Fort is open to visitors only from Memorial Day through Labor Day.

A word about **accomodations:** Because of its hunting and fishing prominence, Devils Lake has several "inns" and "lodges" scattered along its shore. *These are not Holiday Inns*, or anything like them. These are as a rule one- to four-room cabins, often with bunk beds, that cater to mostly male sportsmen. You'll find complete kitchens at these places, but no flat-screen TVs, no hair dryers, and no 400-thread count linens. Many lodges request that you bring your own soap, not to mention shampoo and conditioner. If you're a hunter or an angler, you're probably familiar with this lodging genre and its (low) level of amenities. If you must have an indoor swimming pool and a new mattress, you're better off staying in town at a chain.

Despite the beating it's taken from floods over the years, the Devils Lake area is always worth visiting. Many of those lodges I've just mentioned are open year-round for ice-fishing, cross-country skiing, and snowmobiling. Be sure to check road conditions before you go at **www.dot.nd.gov**.

*Devils Lake Post Office. The ghosts are on the inside.*

# SONS OF JACOB: NOT JUST A CEMETERY

As we mentioned in the Southeastern section (see *North Dakota Dreamers*), there were some early pioneers who ate herring and rye bread, stuffed cabbage and sauerkraut soup, but unlike their Norwegian or German-Russian neighbors did not celebrate Christmas. The Jews who settled in the Devils Lake region also hailed from Russia but were never as numerous or as strong as their coreligionists in the Wishek-Ashley area. We know about the Devils Lake Jews thanks to **Rachel Calof**, who was a "picture" or mail-order bride when she came west in the 1880s. Her book, *Jewish Homesteader on the Northern Plains*, was written at the urging of her children when Rachel was already over 70 years old, and is considered a classic pioneer memoir.

Rachel wastes no words describing the worse than harsh conditions she discovered in North Dakota, and she led a life of endless wrangling with her controlling, superstitious and thoroughly evil mother-in-law. Her bitterest complaints, however, involved her lack of privacy. Rachel and her husband, Jacob, met "on the prairie" when they craved intimacy.

Rachel gave birth in a two-room shack, raised five children, fought injuries and illness and crushing post-partum depression, and *Jewish Homesteader* has been adapted as a one-woman play by seasoned actress Kate Fuglei of Los Angeles: she performed it in Minneapolis to rave reviews in 2013, and hopefully audiences around the country will soon get a chance to see this riveting performance.

All that remains of the Devils Lake community is found at the **Sons of Jacob Cemetery**, on a gravel road off County Road 17 west of Edsmore. At the end of the gravel it's a short walk to the gravesites, atop the only hill around. The cemetery's height, and its bright green grass, make the site stand out among the lighter-colored fields, while at the same time somehow making the gravesites seem even lonelier, perhaps even more isolated.

The engravings, in Hebrew and English, are largely illegible, but the heartbreak is clear: a majority of those interred were under 21, and many are infants or small children. A local citizen, Michael Connor – whose sister, ill with cancer, received help from a Jewish merchant – maintains the place. See *sojnorthdakota.org* for photos, directions and additional information.

JEWISH HOMESTEADERS
CHARLEY ABRAHAM
ABRAHAM ADELMAN
JOSEPH ADELMAN
PIT ALSWANG
ISAAC BECKER
JAKE BERKOWITZ
LEVI BRITSK
ISRAEL BUCHMANN
ABRAM CALOF
MAIER CALOF
BARNETT CANTOR
FRED CANTOR
SIMON CLITCHEN
KATIE COHEN
RUEBEN COHEN
LOUIS COLOSKY
ARON COMONOW
SARAH COMONOW
THEODORE DEKEYZER
IDA U.DELAVECH
ISAAC DELAVECH
ISAAC EDELMAN
SIMON ETTINGER
LASER FILIS
OORA FRANKEL
ARON FRIEDMAN
HERMAN FRIEDMAN
JACOB FRIEDMAN
LENA FRIEDMAN
ZENDA GILMAN
JOSEPH J. GOLDBERG
SAM GOLDBERG
SOLOMON GOLDBERG
SOLOMON GOLDSTEIN
LOUIS GOODERMAN
HEMIS GRAWOIG
ABRAHAM GREENBERG
BEN GREENBERG
MOLLIE GREENBERG
PHILLIP GREENBERG
BENIE GREENBERG
JACOB GROSSMAN
JOSEPH W. GROSSMAN
HERMAN HOFFMAN
DAVID HOLLANDER
MAX HOLLANDER
SAM HOLLANDER
NATHAN HORWITZ
LUIS KAHAN
SAVOL KALOV
SOLOMON KALOV
HERC KAPLON
LOVE KASLOW
ALBERT KAUFMAN
HERMAN KAUFMAN
ABRAHAM KEMPINSKY
SIMON KLIZEN
BINEY KOHN
MAX KOHN
MOSKO KOLOV
ABRAHAM LESCHENSKY
MENDEL LEVITZ
HYMAN LIBERMAN
RACHEL LIEBERMAN
SARAH LIEBERMAN
H. MARGOLIS
LOUIS MAVIL
ISRAEL MILL
MAX MILL
MICHAEL MOSCHITSKA
HEIMS NATHAN
SIMON NATHAN
NUDELMAN
M. OXMAN
CHARLES PARKS
ABRAHAM PENNER
MOSES PLENTNICHKY
IKE PYES
MAX PYES
ABRAHAM RACKNER
SAM ROSENTHAL
ISRAEL M. ROSENWATE
BESSIE RUBIN
DAVIS RUBIN
DAVID SCHAPERA
ISAAC SCHAPERA
JOSEF SCHAPERA
SAMUEL C SCHAPERA
JACOB SCHECTER
HALLECK SCHECTER
ESTHER SCHLEMISON
MAX SCHULMSON
ABRAHAM SHERMAN
WOOLF SHEROWITZ
JACOB SOLOMENSKE
ISAAC SPERIOR
ABE STEREN
HYMAN WALK
S. L. WINEMAN
EMMA WOLFE
JACOB WOLFE
MAX WOLFSON
JOHN YAFFE
JOSEPH ZUNICH

# SPECIAL FEATURE: BLOOD ON THE PRAIRIE

North Dakota has always been one of the safest states in the Union, but these lands have seen their share of violent and horrific acts. Here's a small sampling of some of the more Gothic crimes ever to (dis)grace the state.

- **The Kreider Murders**

Back in 1893, Mennonite settler Daniel Kreider, his wife Barbara, and four of their eight children were slaughtered on their farm near Devils Lake, in a crime that involved transborder flight, a lynching party, and a breakfast from hell.

The motive wasn't robbery, but love. A hired hand, Albert Bomberger, was mad for the oldest daughter, fifteen-year-old Annie. She wasn't interested, to the point of complaining to her father. Daniel Kreider ordered Bomberger off the farm, and at first the hired hand appeared to cooperate. Less than a week later, however, Bomberger showed up at the Kreider home armed with a gun and a knife.

He shot Daniel Kreider at point-blank range in the bedroom, then turned to the kitchen where Barbara stood screaming. She was also shot, before Bomberger cut her throat. Then he turned to the children: Mary, 11, Melby, 9, and 7-year-old David. They were all dead within thirty minutes. At this point Bomberger headed for the barn, where Annie's younger sister, Bernice, 13, had fled when the killing began. Finding Bernice huddled in the straw, Bomberger dragged her back into the house. He took her into the kitchen and made her look at her dead parents before murdering her, in another room.

The other four children – Annie, 5-year-old Aaron, Eva, 4, and Henry, 3 – expected the worst, but Bomberger spared their lives. He demanded that Annie cook him breakfast, in the kitchen where her dead mother lay. He then raped her in the barn before tying her up, hopping on the family's pony and making a beeline for Canada.

Annie displayed remarkable fortitude. Very soon after her brother Aaron untied her, Annie was composed enough to fetch family friend and local merchant Samuel Brightbill to the home. When Brightbill and other neighbors viewed the blood-soaked scene, they decided to form a posse and were soon on Bomberger's trail, making good time. The chase became a race, with the sheriff and the posse, trying to streak past each

64

other on the way to Manitoba. Bomberger was captured, by the sheriff, in that province and returned to the state.

They tried to jail Bomberger in Devils Lake, but the locals were vociferous, gathering outside with guns and a rope. Somehow the sheriff smuggled Bomberger past the mob to a safer haven in Grand Forks. Justice was done: Bomberger was found guilty in lawfully convened court. On January 19, 1894, Bomberger was hung by the neck until he was dead. There is an unauthenticated claim that the scaffold stood on the Kreider property, right outside that kitchen.

The remaining Kreider children, including Annie, returned to their home state of Pennsylvania. The Kreider place was sold to a new owner, but it burned to the ground in 1917, taking its horrible history with it.

## • The Turtle Lake Murders

This small town near the Missouri River saw carnage on April 23, 1920 when eight people, including six members of the Wolf family, met their ends at the hands of one Henry Layer. Layer, proprietor of the next farm over, got into a dispute with Mr. Wolf over his dog. According to Layer, the Wolf pooch was harassing his cattle. Naturally Wolf defended his dog, and soon the guns (and a hatchet) came out. Before long all the Wolfs were dead except the baby, Emma, then eight months old. Layer also killed a Wolf relation and a farmhand only 13 years old.

Layer tried hiding the bodies but eventually confessed. He drew life in prison. No word on what happened to the dog.

## • The Spicer Murders

On achieving statehood, North Dakota outlawed all saloons, and specifically prohibited selling booze to Indians. However, many saloon-keepers defied the law and maintained secret liquor stores known as "blind pigs."

On Valentine's Day of 1897, two Indians near the now-extinct town of Winona made it to what they thought was a "blind pig." The proprietor denied having any alcohol, and he sent them to Mr. Pepper, the town drayman and water hauler. Off went the Indians to the Pepper residence.

Here's where the story veers into dangerous farce. "I've got no liquor," said Mr. Pepper, "but I know where it is. You go on over to the Spicer home – you know Tom Spicer? He's got it. He'll sell it to you."

Pepper must have been chuckling underneath his mustache, because Thomas Spicer and his family were Christian believers, famous in the neighborhood for never touching alcohol. Pepper probably pictured a comedic scene, with the Indians, Frank Black Hawk and Alec Coudotte, demanding hooch from a shocked and outraged Spicer.

Pepper underestimated the Indians. Black Hawk and Coudette picked up three confederates and found Tom Spicer cleaning his barn. After sitting with him and chatting coolly for a few minutes, the visitors shot Spicer in the back and hacked him up with an axe and some farm tools. They then sauntered to the house and told Mary Spicer that her husband was asking for her in the barn. She was shot dead upon arrival, and her body mutilated as well.

For reasons unknown, the five killers picked up a club and went back to the house. There they killed Mary Spicer's aging mother and a Spicer daughter, Lillie Rowse. Mrs. Rowse and her two-year-old twins were staying with her parents while her husband worked elsewhere.

Lillie fought back, whacking Coudotte with a shotgun. Another killer, Paul Holy Track, was clubbed and cut with a broken hoe before the five men overpowered Lillie and killed her, along with her children.

This dreadful crime went undiscovered for a week. A state attorney, H.A. Armstrong, got wind of something wrong at the Spicers' and rode out there on his horse. You can imagine his reaction on discovering six bullet-ridden, mutilated corpses, including the two little children. Eventually all the suspects were arrested, and two, including Paul Holy Track, confessed.

The trial did not go smoothly. One judge was replaced after Coudotte was found guilty and sentenced to a hanging death. The next defendant, George Defender (I am not making up these names), won a mistrial on the first round, and the State Supreme Court found that both Defender and Coudotte merited second trials, despite the confessions.

Local observers were furious. On November 13, 1887, forty men in masks showed up at the jail where Coudotte, Holy Track and defendant Philip Ireland were being held. They managed to overpower the jailer, seize his keys, and bring out the prisoners with ropes around their necks. Three times the mob tried to lynch the three Indians, but it was only on the third attempt that they succeeded, suspending the defendants from a beef windlass on a local farm.

This was the only lynching ever recorded in Emmons County, and one of only nine in the entire state.

This murder, in a fictional form, served as a plot device in Louise Erdrich's novel, *The Plague of Doves.*

- **Oil Patch Killings**

In a contemporary story, Omar Mohammed Kalmio was convicted of murdering his girlfriend and four members of her family in Minot, in 2011.

Kalmio shot Sabrina Zephier, 19, her 13 year old brother, her mother, her sister and the sister's husband at their mobile home. All the Zephiers were Yankton Sioux, while Kalmio is a Somali national.

In his trial, Kalmio's co-workers in the drilling industry stated that Kalmio complained about Sabrina Zephier "trapping" him by getting pregnant and having the baby (a little girl, who was unharmed in the shooting).

Although Kalmio claimed he'd come to the U.S. for political asylum, crime seems to have been present in his life for a long time. Back in 2006, he served a year in prison for stabbing a man in Minneapolis. He also had a theft conviction dating to that year.

Kalmio is now serving a life sentence.

# THE NORTHWEST

*I.    Bottineau – Kenmare – Minot*
*II.    Minot – Williston – "Ghost" Towns of the Northwest*

Drive west out of Bottineau on State Route 5 and wonder at your own insignificance. All North Dakota is big, of course – big farms, big views, and then there's that oversized sky – but up here you will travel furthest from shore on the ocean of the plains. Fargo and Grand Forks might as well be Minneapolis. They might as well be New York; that's how distant and foreign those cities feel up here amid the endless stretch of farmland. America sprawls on your left hand, and somewhere there is squawking and bustle and screech and slam, there are bright orchards, sunny backyards, and way, way down there, three days away, Texas bristling against the border, but you cannot see, hear, feel it. You don't know it. You have risen above. On your right hand, Canada runs in its neat, modest way up to the big lakes, the muskeg, the tundra. You're not there either.

Welcome to northwest North Dakota. You are in, not outer but upper space. There's lots of room. There is serious ag. This is no longer the Midwest: cowboy hats and boots replace brimmed caps and work shoes. You are, though, back in the Prairie Pothole Region, and they've got the lakes to prove it.

In the eighty miles between Bottineau and Kenmare, there are no real towns, only the proverbial wide spots in the road with, maybe, a gas station and convenience store. Abandoned houses crop up here, not many, some still looking livable, others leaning to the southeast where the wind has blown them.

One place that is no longer in daily use yet not abandoned is **Mouse River Lutheran Church**, located on an unnumbered gravel road that runs south 22 miles west of Bottineau. This handsome, high-spired white church first saw worshippers in 1892, and its first class was confirmed in 1905. The congregation survived for one hundred years and then some, but the marquee was last updated back in 2001.

Although it's not possible to enter the church itself, outside a smooth green churchyard tells us who used to live here: Carlsons, Skaggards, Knutsons, Johnsons. Today there are hardly any houses within miles of this church, yet its existence speaks of a time when small farmers and ranchers rode or walked here to commune with their God. As with the

Jewish cemeteries in Ashley and near Devils Lake, this place is being carefully tended. A small dwelling next door may be inhabited – nobody home when we visited – so if you see someone, ask.

*Gravestones at Mouse River Lutheran Church*

One of the gems of this area is the **J. Clark Salyer Wildlife Refuge**. Headquartered two miles north of the town of Upham, the best and perhaps only way to get here is to drive south for approximately eight miles on County Road 14, eight miles west of Bottineau. **Do not attempt to find the refuge entrance north of Highway 5; the only entry is off Highway 14.** Maps may suggest otherwise, but they are flat wrong.

The largest wildlife refuge in the state, Salyer is located on the Mouse, or Souris, River and runs for 45 miles southwest from the Manitoba border. Glacial lakes hundreds of miles in area once covered the region, and the long strip of water that makes up the refuge is one of their remnants. Here you begin to see what hunters smilingly call the "duck factory" of North Dakota: in migrating season, thousands of Donalds and Daisies, and maybe even an Uncle Scrooge, flutter their feathers across the flat expanse of wetlands, sandhills and occasional woodlands. Marvel at the winged ones' iridescent colors and feet in bright shades of yellow, red and orange. Look out for cranes and herons while you're at it, and watch for squadrons of white pelicans moving together like a formation of B-17s. Hiking trails around the marshes shelter upland game birds: in the fall, listen for the drumming of grouse or the sudden flight of a ring-necked pheasant. No hunting here; if you don't believe it, look up the word "refuge."

Further west, a great dip in the road and a flash of blue water announce the Des Lacs River, a wide and improbable waterway eighteen miles from the terminus of Highway 5. There is a wildlife-refuge sign by the river, but don't attempt to enter there unless you have a high-clearance 4-wheel-drive vehicle, as mud is almost guaranteed. This is the Upper Souris Wildlife Refuge, and the way there is south of Kenmare. We'll get to that.

When Highway 5 ends, turn left on State Route 52. This is another one of North Dakota's amazing highways (*see* Great Roads) and runs in an arrow-straight diagonal from northwest to southeast, all the way down to distant Jamestown in I-94.

*Lower Des Lacs Wildlife Refuge in autumn.*

If you are headed to Minot, **Kenmare**, on Highway 52 off Highway 5, is the largest town in the region with almost 1100 people, and the logical place to stop.

There's a red-brick downtown here with a flourishing **Kenmare Drug** and an authentic Danish windmill. Built by an immigrant in 1902, the windmill was restored and moved to its present home in 1959. You can walk through the structure and ponder how the search for renewable energy is nothing new.

Out on Highway 52, a brand-new housing development, incongruous in its bright paint and shiny rooftops, seems like a head-scratcher until you start noticing the semis, one after another, pouring out diesel smoke as they scud by in the left lane, heading south. You are arriving in **the Bakken**, or at least its far-flung suburbs. Fasten your hard hat.

From Kenmare to Minot, around 25 miles, the traveler skates on a thin but enchanting strip of Highway 52 through a narrow valley between high bluffs to the east, marking the edge of the Missouri Escarpment, and pine-dotted badlands, or near-badlands, on the right. It's as if you'd skipped from Nebraska to Montana in one jump.

While on this route, don't fail to turn off at **Carpio**, a peaceful green spot along the Des Lacs River which is the gateway to the **Upper Souris Wildlife Refuge**. Magnificent views and an abundance of birds are your rewards, and although the highway is just a few miles and an overpass away, you'll enjoy delightful isolation from the refuge's hilltop viewing sites.

North Dakota is full of surprises, and here's one more: the tiny town of **Des Lacs**, hugging the Burlington Northern line off a gravel road around 8 miles west of Minot, made feminist history back in 1922, when the citizens elected women, and only women, to every post in town. East Coast papers wrote up the event and the colorful torchlight parade around City Hall, which would have been nice if there was a City Hall in Des Lacs at the time, which there wasn't. Still, this story illustrates one more way in which North Dakota has always defied stereotypes and easy assumptions.

## MINOT

Like other North Dakota cities, Minot feels bigger than it really is. Stay there for a few days, and it'll come as a shock to learn that, with a population of some 36,000, the city is smaller than metropoli like Bountiful, Utah or Goose Creek, South Carolina. Minot has a skyline, a multi-story downtown, a flourishing chain-store strip just south of town, and the North Dakota State Fairgrounds, which draw people not just during fair season in July but all year long for many types of events of national, local, and international interest.

"International?" you say, with a slight sneer. We reply to you, Oh *yaaa*. When companies and craftsfolk from five European countries descend on Minot every year, that is plenty international. I'm talking, of course, about **Norsk Høstfest**, the five-day celebration of all things Scandinavian that draws literally tens of thousands from across the U.S. and Canada in early October (see below). The Fairgrounds, which encompass six exhibition halls, historic sites, and parking lots to rival Disneyland's, is home as well to everything from car shows and craft venues to a mass cook-off, in which volunteers prepare, cook and package up to 500,000 meals to be shipped overseas for needy families.

Minot beckons to shoppers from all over North Dakota, but especially the underserved northwestern part of the state. In addition to the big-box chains (i.e., Sears, J.C. Penney's, Target and Walmart), many independent boutiques serve the general and niche markets. In downtown, **Bray's Saddlery** (215 S. Main Street, 838-1705) fulfills your Western cravings with a full line of boots, snap-front shirts, hats and horse trappings. **Dakota Antiques and Books** (3 1st St. SE, 838-1150) has an excellent assortment of new and used books along with toys, pioneer artifacts, paper products and more. Purists may want to opt for **Main Street Books** (106 S. Main, 839-4050), a fiercely independent bookstore that features local and regional authors and does not allow price-comparison apps to be used on their premises. Stores like this give a town character; if you like North Dakota, and you want to keep downtowns alive, you'll want to wander in, graze the shelves, and buy something.

## Sleep

Hotels in Minot are mostly clustered around the south end strip, and new ones go up, it seems, every hour. This book liked the **Candlewood Suites** (900 37th Avenue SW, 858-7700), a blocklike fortress on the outside like so many newer hostelries, but comfortably furnished and graced with full kitchens in every room. All the well-known chains are represented, along with regional favorites like **AmericInn** and **Cobblestone**. Prices are reasonable, even during festivals and busy times of year.

## Eat & Drink

Dining well is easy here. At the top of the list there's **10 North Main** (10 N. Main Street, 837-1010), arguably a celebrity hangout since one of the owners is heartthrob actor **Josh Duhamel**, a North Dakota native. Local pheasant is the big-deal menu item, but all manner of game (including elk) appears on the menu, along with steaks, pastas and an exceptional wine list. Buffalo strip steaks win raves, and French onion soup is perfect on a cold or rainy day. Desserts are appropriately fabulous, and although the price tag is steepish for the state, there's no better place in town for celebrations and that big-city feel.

Another popular choice is **Big Time Bistro** (101 Central Avenue West, 839-2666). Outstanding sandwiches and homemade chips are among the mainstays at this independently-owned eatery (with pub next door). There are no waiters, so your reaction may depend on how you feel about picking up your own order. Music videos playing on the walls thrill some, but if you don't care for that sort of thing, you might check other places. Still, this is a great lunch stop.

Italian food is on hand at **Michael's** (515 20th Avenue SE, 837-6133) and at **Primo Grand International** (1505 N. Broadway, 852-3161).

**Baan Rao Thai** (401 40thSt SE, 839-5508) satisfies pad thai and beef satay cravings. **Mi Mexico** (301 40<sup>th</sup> Avenue SW, 858-0777) has a charming atmosphere, colorful murals and friendly service, although the food is far from *autentico* (but then, we are far from Mexico here).

Elsewhere in Minot, chain restaurants by the truckload serve those who crave the familiar, and no less than seven coffeehouses (only one of them a **Starbuck's**) pour the necessary beverage.

## SCANDINAVIAN HERITAGE PARK

If you need to get into a pre-Høstfest mood, or if you've already been and want to learn more, don't forget to stop at **Scandinavian Heritage Park** (1020 S. Broadway, 852-9161). This is a broad and beautiful spot in downtown Minot that honors all five Scandinavian nations and features a life-sized replica of a 13<sup>th</sup> century wooden church.

The **Gol Stave Church Museum** is a remarkable structure, identical in every detail to the original built in Gol, in the Hallingdal region of Norway, around 1250. That church was moved to an Oslo museum around 100 years ago, but the North Dakota version was dedicated in 1999. A local doctor, Myron Peterson, M.D., organized the committee and helped gather the funds to raise the building. With hand-carved wooden doors and portals, the church-museum is a stunning tribute to the pioneers who left a wind-scarred, snow-filled landscape for ... another much like it, only without the mountains, the tyrannous king, and the sparse, rocky soil. In traditional Norwegian belief, the four corners of the church represent the four Gospels, the roof beams stand in for the apostles, and the floor boards, in an exuberant flight of faith-based fancy, symbolize humble folks, who despite being trampled on provide support to the congregation. The swooping roof is a practical, snow-shedding design, but it too has spiritual significance, personifying those whose prayers keep sin at a distance.

The **eternal flame** was literally carried to Minot from Morgedal, Norway in 1993. Honoring Sondre Norheim, who helped popularized skiing around the world, five stylized skis surrounding the flame represent the five nations (Norway, Sweden, Denmark, Iceland and Finland, in case you were wondering) and support a globe attesting to skiing's ascendancy as a global sport.

The 30-foot high **Dala Horse** is an outsize representation of bright-colored, hand-carved wood horses created by Swedish artisans since around 1840. Originally meant as toys for children, Dala (pronounced "Dawla") horses came into being as a way of spending those long winter nights: free time, plus a knife, plus a regional history of furniture-making which meant lots of scrap wood lying around, and presto, there's your horsie, Lasse. Characteristic of Dala horses are the flower-painted harness and saddle designs.

In summer, the **Nordic Pavilion for the Arts** is home to open-air concerts where traditionally-dressed Sons of Norway serve up traditionally delicious Nordic treats. The pavilion's dedication, in 2003, featured music by the Scandinavian Accordion Club of New York, no less, and you may hold your wedding or other celebration at the Pavilion if you like (contact the park for more information).

There's much more at this park, including a waterfall, a pioneer house, a Finnish sauna and a Danish windmill, so plan on spending the best part of your day here, if you go. Admission is free.

# NORSK HØSTFEST

The brochure promises "Scandimonium," and at this, perhaps the state's largest and certainly its best-known annual event, the party atmosphere is nonstop. Of course, this is a *Scandinavian* party, so if you're looking for strippers, streakers and street frolics, Mardi Gras it ain't. On the other hand, you will probably never again see so many tall, blond people wearing patterned sweaters in one place. You will never smell so much cinnamon and cardamom. You may never again get the chance to eat delicacies like Uff-Da Tacos and Finnish beef stews and fried walleye sandwiches. The pastries are to die for, the craft booths are fascinating, and the entertainment –yes, this is also a concert venue – plentiful.

Many hotels offer shuttles directly to the Fairgrounds during Høstfest, but it may be simpler just to drive there, park and ride the festival's rickety school buses to the entrance halls. **Remember where you've parked** – the color and the number – so you can get on the right shuttle bus coming back.

Even on the bus, travelers may get the feeling they've walked into a massive, multi-country family reunion. Everybody seems to know everybody else, and an atmosphere of friendly ribbing dominates the repartee between driver and passengers. You can buy tickets at the door, or order them online. In 2013 admission cost $36 for adults, and it's worth it: much of the entertainment is free, and there are seven, count 'em, seven exhibit halls with stuff to see and do. Knock the plague fleas off the Norway rat? Of course you can! Watch tribute groups run through your favorite artist's best songs? Step right up! Buy scarves, sweaters, hand-made jewelry, books, CDs, artwork, coffee mugs with clever sayings and Norskish holiday décor? Yes, yes, yes, and yes. At night, big-name artists put on full-length concerts for an extra charge, and fans descend en masse to hear acts like Kris Kristofferson (of Danish descent) and Alabama (of Alabaman descent).

Høstfest is a chance to see the largest ethnic group in North Dakota kick up its black-booted heels and live a little. Unlike their, ah, teutonic cousins to the south, Scandinavians have quite a sense of humor and enjoy poking fun at themselves. If you haven't heard any good Ole and Lena jokes lately, get ready for an earful.

Always held the first week of October, Norsk Hostfest concerts sell out first, so visit **www.høstfest.com** to view what's coming up next year.

*Scand-alous!*

# ON FRACKING

## WILLISTON

From Minot, continue west on Highway 2 and prepare for a wild ride. Since 2008, the world has been turning upside down and staying that way, up here in the northwestern part of the state. Whatever you may think of hydraulic fracturing – "fracking," to most of us – there's no doubt that this process, which involves forcing water and other liquids into oil- and gas-bearing shale, has changed and is changing this formerly sleepy corner of the state.

Williston, where Highway 2 meets Highway 85, is Ground Zero for the energy boom. Since 2008, when fracking became economically variable, the area has exploded like nobody's business. Here's where McDonald's pays $18. an hour, where families are sleeping in fifth-wheel travel trailers and where "man camps" – clusters of basic dorms or mobile homes, often with cafeterias, rec rooms and other facilities – have sprung up like boils on the face of the earth, because all these oil men and women need places to stay. Every hotel chain you could think of is represented here, and there's more building happening as time goes by. If you have a truck driver's license, you're wanted in Williston. Huge tanker-trailers run 24/7 from the oil sites to, well, everywhere. It's a strange sight, ugly, awe-inspiring, and not a little thrilling, as you realize that in economic terms it's like looking at San Francisco in 1849, or New York in 1900, or California just after the Second World War.

Coming in from the east, you'll see the land around Williston opening up to a chaotic scene. Here and there bright flames are flaring, methane and other gases being burnt off by the frackers. Oil-seeking derricks look like rocket launchers, but these are built to go down, not up. Squat round towers, shrunken versions of the grain elevators you see elsewhere in the state, huddle together in groups of four, representing storage for the liquids involved. Bobcats and bulldozers push the earth around, while rising from gullies and cascading down hills are new homes and buildings, seemingly four or five per hour. On U.S. 2, which here forms Williston's main drag, traffic comes to a shivering stop. These roads were not meant for constant truck traffic; prepare for lots of "Go Slow" and "Stop" signs wearily hoisted aloft by state workers.

Talk to folks in Williston, and you'll hear some interesting tales. Contractors can't find workers to nail drywall; the siren song of big bucks lures the young men out to oil sites. Man-camp companies duke it out, each promising better food or faster internet in an effort to snag entire companies of crews. Schools are bursting, with the state government shelling out money as fast as it is minted to provide more classrooms, teachers, textbooks and science labs.

# MANCAMPS – HOME OR HELL?

Where you gonna put 'em – all those people, that is, who show up to work in North Dakota, dreaming of oil-field riches? Lodging of every kind is popping up like daffodils in springtime, but for too many workers, a place to stay still means somebody else's couch or floor, or an rental RV plopped down in a field.

This being America, savvy entrepreneurs are on the spot, offering warmer and gentler accommodations complete with 24-hour cafeterias, game and TV rooms, sports facilities and more. Target Enterprises, an early leader in the field, has built barracks-style facilities in Williston and Watford City. Bakken Residences defies that trend with individual cabins that look more at home on the prairie. Whichever a worker (or his employer) chooses, the rules are pretty much the same: no drinking, no drugs, no loud music and no fighting. Female guests (they're not called "man" camps for nothing) are mostly frowned upon, although recently some complexes have opened up to couples. Kids are still a no-no, though.

While there's no denying that some man camp projects are ugly and a blot on the landscape, farmers and ranchers are philosophical about the trend. Why shouldn't they be? Renting to man-camp operators can be just as lucrative – and lots less work – than raising crops or animals.

Exit the madness by heading north on U.S. 85 back to State 5, where in 2010 **Crosby** topped the list of cities in Divide County with a whopping 1,070 residents. It's grown since then; no one knows by how much, but you can see the area changing with construction, especially of houses and hotels. The city's Housing Authority has been busily remodeling apartments and adding low-income housing since 2008, although there is still no such thing as a bar that serves liquor in town.

Head west on Route 5 to a trio of depopulated villages, Ambrose, Fortuna and Alkabo. **Fortuna**'s residents boast that the boom is happening here, as the population has zoomed from 17 to 30 since 2008. Thirsty travelers will cheer the fact that Fortuna has a tavern, although much of its landscape consists of usedtabes: "this usedtabe the gas station ... that usedtabe the elementary school," etc.

**Ambrose** is listed in *Ghosts of North Dakota*, by Troy Larsen and Terry Hinnenkamp (**http://www.ghostsofnorthdakota.com**), an invaluable book with fantastic photos of towns going and gone. However, the 18 residents here dispute the ghostly label, pointing to the fact that the town celebrated its centennial in 2006. In fact, when rural residents are added to the total, there must be at least 40 people who call Ambrose home. Enthusiastic local historians have compiled volumes of local lore, from first-person oral histories to century-old newspaper clippings, documenting life in this "cleft of the world," as Nebraska author Willa Cather described small, unknown places.

For the ultimate in out-of-the-way, however, you should visit **Alkabo** (pronounced Al-KAY-bo), eleven miles from the Montana line. Even the authors of *Ghosts of North Dakota* described this place as "the most remote town we have ever visited," and visitors may feel equally dissociated from the modern world in this place where indoor plumbing has never existed, where municipal utilities are unknown and where the Alkabo school, while on the National Register of Historic Sites, hasn't had a pupil since 1963. As in Ambrose and other tiny towns, however, local residents have established an online community and spend much time reminiscing about the school's merry-go-round, Christmas plays and *lutefisk* suppers catering to the Norwegian-American community. Trains still pass through here, and sometimes visitors come just to set up a chair in the grass and listen to the whistle blow. This is the essence of rural North Dakota.

About ten miles south of Alkabo is **Writing Rock State Historic Site**, home to two huge boulders bearing Indian pictographs of bison, thunderbirds, people and other animals real and imagined. Strange as it may seem today, some early settlers were so incapable of believing these carvings to have been done by Indians that they attributed them to a variety of groups: Vikings, Chinese, even the Ten Lost Tribes of Israel. Now, of course, the thunderbird is almost synonymous with early Indian art, and similar stones have been found in comparatively nearby places such as Alberta, Saskatchewan and Billings, Montana. There are two stones here, thankfully protected behind wire from graffitists and other vandals. This is a great place to stop for a picnic, as there are tables in a grove of trees and under shelters. The kids, and the adults, can use the restrooms before they get back into the car. Admission is always free, but be sure to check conditions: the last few miles into the site is gravel and could wreak havoc on a rental car.

After Writing Rock, continue south on pavement to the link-up with State Route 50 and go east. You'll pass **Grenora**, whose Italianate name is actually drawn from the GReat NOrthern RAilroad, which once upon a time roared through here. Grenora is a thriving small town with schools, an RV park, and annual celebrations.

Going east on Route 50, the traveler finds a string of semi-spectral towns ranging from **Appam** to **Zahl**. While none of these are exactly bustling, there's still a post office at Zahl and eager-beaver realtors are advertising lots for sale. The oil industry has put one of its man camps near Appam, which means that workers and their families are now discovering the endless vistas and onetime homesteads of this underpopulated portion of the state. Don't miss the classic white prairie church in Zahl and the marked sites in Appam including the one-time dancehall.

South on 85 and east on 2, it's twenty-two miles to **White Earth** on the White Earth River. Here a German-language newspaper thrived from 1902 to 1920, but the real draw is a trio of lakes along a gravel road, north from White Earth to the town of Powers Lake. **Cottonwood Lake**, in the middle, has a boat ramp and you can find fishing reports online at **http://www.lake-link.com/**. The gravel ends at Route 50, and seventeen miles east is the **Lostwood National Wildlife Refuge**. Like most wildlife refuges in the state, this one is mostly water and provides cover for migrating and native bird species. No hunting is permitted at the refuge.

# SPECIAL FEATURE:
## FAMOUS NATURAL DISASTERS

Water, concentrated in snowflakes or spread out in floods, has been the culprit in almost all of the state's natural nightmares. Read about these here (preferably in the summer under hot sun).

- **Schoolhouse Blizzard**

One of the nastiest tricks in North Dakota's weather playbook involves a sudden warm spell, a midwinter thaw that brings the children out and gets coats tossed carelessly aside, followed in blindingly swift time by a precipitous drop in the temperature and a raging snowstorm. That's what happened on January 12, 1888. Although there'd been a heavy snowfall only a few days before, heavy enough to keep kids home and stores closed, the mercury climbed to near 40 degrees Fahrenheit early on January 12. Bored kids begged to go to school, and farm folk ventured into town to do their shopping.

By noon it was 20 below and the snow came, whipped by wind. White-out conditions were almost instant, and those who'd left home were soon stranded. Sensible teachers kept the kids in the schoolhouse; those who didn't sent the children out to almost certain death. In all, 235 people died over a three-day period.

- **BLIZZARD OF 1920**

While the blizzard of '88 took more lives, the 1920 blizzard was just as heartbreaking. By this time there were telephones, but all the lines in the state went down (except one, from Fargo to Minneapolis). Once again, schoolchildren were among the victims.

The best-known story is that of 15-year-old Hazel Miner. Stranded with her younger siblings beneath an overturned sleigh in a ravine, Hazel talked to them, kept them awake and sheltered them with her own body. Hazel did not survive the storm, but Emmet, 10, and Myrdith, 8, did. Her selflessness and resourcefulness have been celebrated in songs and books, and North Dakota school kids today routinely read Hazel's story.

Less well-known, perhaps because it is sadder, is the tale of the four

Wohlk brothers, ages 9 through 13. They were the only kids to turn up at their school on that day. When they left the storm was at its height, but the children thought they could make it home, only two miles away. Their horses floundered, and Adolph, the eldest, left to find help.

His body was recovered ¼ mile from home, and the boys' father found the wagon some time later. None survived.

*Hazel Miner.*
*How many teenagers would give their lives to protect their brother and sister?*
*photo courtesy of Center Republican, Center, N.D.*

- **Fargo Tornado - 1957**

North Dakota for the most part is not considered part of "Tornado Alley," that wide swath of vulnerable territory that ranges northeast from Texas to Michigan. Fargo and its environs, however, fall just at the edge of the Alley, and from time to time there have been funnel clouds on the horizon.

The deadliest of these came on June 20, 1957. A very hot day at the beginning of the summer, it was so muggy that Ray Jensen, the National Weather Bureau meteorologist on duty guessed there would be thunderstorms later, and he was right. At his office within the Fargo Airport, Dr. Jensen projected several possible severe-thunderstorm scenarios, including the possibility of a tornado.

Theory turned to reality not long after 6 P.M. A tornado warning was announced, and Dr. Jensen was kept busy answering the public telephone in his office as residents sought information on the storm. At 6:25 he spotted the telltale trailing funnel on the western horizon, located in the vicinity of Casselton and heading east toward Fargo. This tornado "skipped," touching the ground around four times before retreating back into the cloud. As the thunderstorms continued and intensified, Dr.

Jensen knew Fargo was not out of the woods yet, and he was at the window when another funnel emerged from the clouds and touched down.

This second tornado, instead of "skipping," soon grew very wide at the bottom, indicating it was causing destruction over a large area. Dr. Jensen continued calling in updates until his power went out. In the interim period, he saw the debris cloud climb halfway up the funnel and saw "whole sides of houses being thrown 3-4 hundred feet into the air ... just like when you are twirling something and the string breaks." That was the Golden Ridge subdivision, a new area just west of Fargo and the hardest hit by the storm.

Over a thousand houses were damaged, with 329 destroyed outright, some swept clear off their foundations. Ten people did not survive the storm, but the toll would have been much higher if not for Dr. Jensen's close observations and early warnings to evacuate.

# THE SOUTHWEST

*I.  Lewis & Clark Historic Sites and Forts – Stanton – Knife River – Beulah – Zap – Killdeer – Little Missouri State Park*

*II.  Watford City – Theodore Roosevelt National Park, North Unit – Medora – Theodore Roosevelt National Park, South Unit -- Dickinson*

*III.  Bismarck – Fort Abraham Lincoln – On-A-Slant Village – Standing Rock*

Note: west and southwest of the Missouri River you will segue from Central to Mountain Time, an hour earlier winter and summer.

Leaving Minot, the traveler faces a wealth of delightful choices. Besides U.S. 2, winding its way through the heart of the oil shale on its route to Williston and then into Montana, there's the option of U.S. 52, an unusual road in that it is a diagonal heading almost directly southeast until its terminus at Jamestown. Sadly, we were unable to travel that road and it cannot be covered here; we hope to get to it in subsequent editions of this book.

The most obvious route out of Minot is south on U.S. 83, which as we may have said before stretches all the way from Del Rio, Texas to the Canadian border, where it becomes Canadian Route 83. This is a four-lane, high-speed highway which nevertheless offers broad views in every direction and is not completely clogged with Bakken traffic. The road flows south, arrow-straight, until it fetches up against the Big Bend of the Missouri, here dammed into Lake Sakakawea, at **Coleharbor**. That last name signifies wishful thinking on the part of mine interests, who back in the early 20th century hoped to turn their town into a major coal-shipping port. Didn't happen: in 2012, Coleharbor's population was 82. For unknown reasons, this area seems to be slightly more tornado-prone than the rest of western North Dakota, with the last sizable twisters in 1958.

**Lake Sakakawea** itself is an enormous spread of water with 1500 miles of shoreline. Popular with fishermen, the lake features concrete boat ramps located strategically all along its stretch, with **Fort Stevenson State Park** just one of its many hiking and camping areas. On its other side, U.S. 83 passes the Fort Mandan State Historical Site and a Lewis and Clark Interpretive Center before tiny route 200A sidles off to the west. In March, 2014, discussions were under way concerning the possible return of local lands taken by the federal government in the 1950s, for the purpose of building Garrison Dam, to Indian groups and private citizens.

### Lewis and Clark Interpretive Center

Here, visitors are greeted by huge steel statues of the two explorers along with their Mandan friend, Chief Big White. Inside, try on the original natural-fiber garment of the upper Plains, also known as a buffalo robe. Check out the canoe made from a streamside cottonwood tree, just like the ones the Corps constructed during their winter stay. There's a baby backboard, and you can imagine Sakakawea patiently hauling *le petit* Jean-Batiste over the continent on its sturdy frame.

In addition to its Lewis & Clark collection, the interpretive center focuses on the steamboat trade up and down the Missouri after the building of Fort Clark in 1830. This is the museum's newest feature, and it's an eye-opener for those of us a bit hazy on what happened to this area after 1806.

### Fort Mandan Overlook State Historic Site

Nine miles up the river, this is where you can actually see Lewis and Clark's winter stomping grounds. Don't look for the fort itself; Big Muddy floods washed that away long, long ago. Instead, put on your Indiana Jones hat and peer into the archaeological dig begun in 1991 and carried on by the State Historical Society. They haven't uncovered any walls or buildings yet, but you can see a gunflint, some lead shot, and glass beads used as currency among the Indians. **Huff Indian Village** displays many artifacts dating to the 1400s when more than a hundred lodges stood here amid gardens that grew squash, beans and corn. Call 328-3666 for more information (year-round, no admission charge).

Right around here is **Cross Ranch State Park**, a worthy destination for every traveler. **Cross Ranch** isn't easy to find, and GPS can be erratic in these parts. The park's web site directs visitors to a paved road "12 miles south of Hensler," a tiny speck on Route 200A. If you can find Hensler, you can find the brown signs that lead directly to the park. It's also possible to get there by driving six miles south of Hensler on gravel:

possible, but not recommended for passenger cars, especially if there has been recent rain or snow. **Do not let maps fool you into thinking there is an entrance directly from U.S. 83**. There isn't. That way lies heartache, discord and wasted time. Turn west on 200A and don't blink, or you might miss Hensler.

Once there, Cross Ranch makes up in scenery and (comparative) comfort for all the hassle involved in accessing it. Here you can see the Missouri as Lewis and Clark did, no small matter considering all those dams to the north and south. Drive in through the shaded, appealing campsites to the water's edge, and contemplate the low, bone-colored cliffs on the opposite shore as if you, too, wore self-made buckskins and rough moccasins. The beauty of this site is that, look where you may up and down the river from this spot, you will not see evidence of the last two centuries. The place is raw and vital and mysterious, not necessarily suited for postcards but evocative beyond belief. The willows and cottonwoods that fringe all watercourses in the state have here matured into a deciduous forest of green ash, box elder and American elm, with some bur oak mixed in. Deer are common, bald eagles put in an appearance from time to time, and endangered species such as whooping cranes, piping plovers and least terns alight and perch on sandbars in the river.

This park has followed current fashion and put up some **yurts** in the park. Yurts, canvas-covered round tents that are Mongolian in origin, contain wood-burning stoves for windy and chilly nights and are ideal for those who'd like to camp but detest hauling and setting up gear. Although visitors will need to bring their own linens and utensils, restrooms including showers are close by and there are outdoor grills for cooking. Best of all, the yurts are located only a stone's throw from the river. At night you can hear the current rushing by and know that you are truly removed from what passes, these days, for civilization. Contact the park at 791-3731 for more information, but use the state parks web site to make a reservation.

From Cross Ranch, continue west on Route 2001 until the junction with State Highway 48, where another archeological site beckons.

*When is a tent not a tent? When it's a yurt!*
*Cross Ranch State Park.*

**Fort Clark State Historic Site**

Here is another ongoing archaeological dig (May 16-September 15, 328-3508, free admission), investigating the Mandan and Hidatsa tribes as well as the trading posts that coexisted with them. We have first-hand accounts of life here, thanks to the journal kept by one Francis A. Chardon. By this time, steamboats were hurrying up and down the river, keeping the fort and the trading post well supplied with trade goods. Unfortunately, when the *St. Peters* tied up to the dock on June 14, 1837, the smallpox bacillus came on shore with one of the crewman, and the result was a decimation that would claim 800 lives before autumn set in. There were bungled attempts at inoculation, all matter of phantom "cures," and no end of horrific stories, including the death of Chardon's own two year old son. Suicides were rampant, affecting whites and Indians equally.

Today, the haunting remains of what was a thriving community are slowly coming to light as scientists and volunteers painstakingly sift through the mud and debris. Aerial photographs clearly show the circles that denote individual lodges, and their outlines may also be traced on the ground. Fort Clark serves as another grisly reminder of how cruel life could be before modern medicine.

Leave Fort Clark S.H.S. and continue west until Route 200A becomes simply Route 200, and head for **Stanton**. A few miles south of the junction between Route 200 and State Route 31, enjoy lunch or dinner at the delightful **Café Dumond** (745-3545), set back from the road under broad-trunked cottonwoods. This is an authentic small-town, local-oriented café with friendly service and tasty food (the chiliburger came open face, on a platter, and was delicious). Expect conversation with your fellow diners who can fill you in on Stanton's history and current doings, and enjoy the many clever French touches on the menu and in the décor: the Parisian-styled ladies room is a hoot. Across the street, seemingly close enough to touch, loaded coal trains chug and whiz by: ask a local to point out the coal company power plant on a nearby hill.

From Stanton, it's just a short drive north on Highway 31 to **Knife River Indian Villages State Historic Site** (see *Best of North Dakota*). This is by far the largest and most comprehensive of the sites clustered along the bend of the Missouri, and its location affords the best views.

### Knife River Indian Villages State Historic Site

This was the home of the Hidatsa, the tribe that kidnapped Sakakawea from her home in the Rocky Mountains. This was one case of a bad deed begetting good ones: if Sakakawea had not been kidnapped (and most of her family killed), she would not have met and married the French Canadian trader, Charbonneau. If she had not married Charbonneau, who could speak several Indian languages, she would never have gone west with Lewis and Clark, and they might never have crossed the Rockies, let alone reach the Pacific.

Today Knife River commemorates the Hidatsa, who numbered some 3000 people in 1804. Although decimated by the smallpox epidemics of the 1830s as described above, the Hidatsa, Mandan and Arikara continue to carry on their traditional basketweaving, beading and leatherwork. Somehow they also find time to run the **4 Bears Casino**, their new gaming yacht on the river.

Walk the well-marked trail, about a mile, down to the Knife, a tributary of the Missouri. Wooden steps have been placed into the hillside, but be careful in wet or muddy weather. Here you get a good idea of what George Catlin painted back in the 1830s, before the awful smallpox epidemic that laid waste to the Mandan. Look for the round depressions in the grass, each marking the spot where a lodge once stood. Apparently at this place the Mandan packed their lodges so closely together that there was barely space to spread a drying rack (for skins) between them.

Best of all are the intact lodges maintained by the Park Service, which you can actually enter in season. Like Dr. Who's Tardis, a Mandan lodge is bigger on the inside, and there's room enough for several families to shelter inside those earthen walls. Notice the exceptionally stout and strong center poles, and the top opening through which smoke blew away. Some of the lodges are equipped with ceremonial items like beaded medicine bags and clay pipes; the Indians mined the clay far from here, in the southeast corner of the state. On sunny days, the lodge was a cool retreat, and on wet or cold days, it provided shelter, warmth and companionship.

The land itself is important here. An ongoing **Native Prairie**

**Restoration** at Knife River demonstrates how scientists are working to eradicate invasive species and reestablish native ones. Plan your day carefully, as these places have a way of making a half-hour stay stretch into half a day (*year-round, free, 745-3300*).

One convenient place to spend the night is the bustling coal town of **Beulah**, on County Route 49 around three miles south of Route 200. Like many places in North Dakota, Beulah is growing and new lodgings are going up all the time. The **AmericInn** (2100 2nd Avenue Northwest, 873-2220) is among these, set up on a hill almost by itself. An indoor pool and Jacuzzi relax the road-weary, and there's an attractive fitness room. Bathrooms run to granite countertops and separate shampoo and conditioner bottles, always a pleasant touch. There is an elevator, and a small refrigerator in each room. While the "closet" is only a few sets of hooks on the wall, the shower provides a movable rain-style head, and the lobby beats most chains for charm and an inviting quality. Meet there in the morning for the usual mostly-hot breakfast free of charge.

If you land at the AmericInn at dinnertime and don't feel like driving, toddle across the parking lot to the newly opened **Fanatics Sports Bar** (873-2143). You'll find truckloads of single men, mostly young, stubblefaced and dressed for the blue-collar jobsite (unlike so many other young men, these guys actually have a jobsite to go to). After dark they come here to relax and cheer their favorite teams on the bar's multiple TV screens. The food is good and reasonable, and even mildly healthy: my chicken-salad sandwich came with that local rarity, a side salad. Service is fast and brewskys can be humungous: ask for the 25-ouncer if you're absolutely, positively not going to drive.

Speaking of jobsites, Beulah's economy runs on a triad of interesting industries. Dakota Gasification takes locally occurring lignite coal and turns it into gas. Two electrical stations, Coyote and Antelope Valley, provide power for Beulah's bright lights, and coal producing companies have been hauling black stuff from the ground since the 1920s.

From this point, you're less than sixty miles from some of the most visited parts of North Dakota – which are also some of the most scenic and historic, of course. Route 200 from Beulah to the junction with U.S. 85 steers travelers to and around a series of vistas that are typically North Dakotan, in other words, varied. From coal-seamed mounding hills that resemble Pennsylvania (okay, without the trees) to great flats where eerie gas flares announce the presence of the Bakken, to red rocks and twisted junipers like Arizona's, this is a study in the contrasts of the state.

Only a few miles from Beulah is **Zap**. This place was established as a lignite strip mine, although thankfully no stripped earth is visible from the road. As far back as the 1930s, the mines produced almost 150,000 tons of coal per year. Today, however, Zap is better known for the **Zip to Zap** spring-break promotion/riots of May, 1969 (see *North Dakota's Woodstock?*). From here the road follows the Spring River to the northwest, and oil extracting outfits start appearing.

Pause for a moment and take in the view. From Highway 200, cut into the side of the coal hills, you look down across fields of wheat and sunflowers to the clusters of large, basic buildings with their backs to the Knife River. Trucks maneuver around parking lots, tiny workers come and go, and at the end of every complex there's that bright flare, the unnatural glowing of natural gas. While state authorities and oil companies are presently working together to reduce the flares' presence, right now they still illuminate the business of a state whose percentage of millionaires jumped by 53 percent from 2012 to 2014.

Past the junction with County Route 8, Horse Nose Butte rears up at nearly 2500 feet, and you know you are in the real West. Ridge after rising ridge heaps up in front of you, and there is color in the rock. Sunflowers grow here, their brilliance dazzling the eye in July, their enormous drooping heads wide as pumpkins in the fall. **Lake Ilo National Wildlife Refuge** appears: here scientists discovered proto-Indian relics, dating back to the last ice age. The road begins to rise as you enter hilly **Killdeer**.

# ZIP TO ZAP – NORTH DAKOTA'S OWN WOODSTOCK?

Frustrated with the high cost of spring-break party travel, NDSU students in the spring of 1969 organized and publicized what they named "Zip to Zap, A Grand Festival of Light and Love." One ad in the Bison newspaper *The Spectrum* led to interest and responses from as far away as Florida and Texas. The media, already giddy with hysteria over student protests on the coasts and elsewhere, picked up the story; aided by alliteration's appeal, news outlets and anchors up to the redoubtable Walter Cronkite zoomed in on Zip to Zap.

Local residents thought the concept was *far out*. Mayor Norman Fuchs declared the city of 250 open to welcome all comers, and Main Street merchants eagerly awaited business. On May 9, the kids started arriving.

This being North Dakota, a long way from Berkeley or Columbia, beer was the intoxicant of choice. Soon drunk people in their late teens and their early twenties began to do what drunk people of that age inevitably do: vomit, fight and fall down, not necessarily in that order. This being North Dakota, it became quite cold at night, and the student-built bonfire on Main Street was in violation of town laws. As almost always happened in those days, the National Guard was called in, bleary-eyed students shouted at impassive soldiers, and a downtown café was completely trashed. TV news ran the story on May 10 as their number one item.

Zip to Zap was the only "riot" in North Dakota's history.

William E. (Bill) Shemorry Photograph Collection

*"He built a fire on Main Street/ And shot it full of holes."* – Bob Dylan

**Killdeer** is in rodeo country, and the PRCA arena is one of the biggest draws in town. With falsefront buildings lining a narrow Main Street, Killdeer is a pointed reminder of how much Old West authenticity remains, ungilded and unyuppified, in North Dakota. The **Buckskin Bar and Grill** (64 Central Avenue S, 764-5321) doesn't have swinging doors, but the ambience is definitely saloon-like. Try the chicken corn chowder when the wind is high and cold. Although the town proudly bills itself as "Cowboy Country," a major oil field less than twenty miles west of here reminds visitors of the 21$^{st}$ century.

Killdeer's foremost attraction, however, is firmly rooted in the Western past. The **Medicine Hole** is a series of cave openings now on private land, into which 200 Sioux warriors and their families reportedly escaped during one of Gen. Alfred Sully's frequent punitive raids on the tribes during the 1860s. Sully knocked off Indians the way cats knock off mice, which is to say often and without mercy. After one battle in 1864, a band of Indians, surrounded on a hillside, apparently disappeared without a trace (Sully is said to have encountered them again, miles away, some weeks later). About all that can be said for certain is that the caves exist, and that winds have emerged from them, suggesting the possibility of more caves that may open up in undisclosed locations. For some time clueless tourists amused themselves by dropping stones into the hole, just to hear them clunk at a distant, unseen bottom; eventually, as you might have guessed, several holes filled up and the caves are now considered impassable.

To get there, look for Mile Marker 110 off Highway 22 north of Killdeer. Turn west and follow a  bumpy road to an unimproved campground (no water) and a path up the side of the hill to the Hole's location. Don't even think of trying to climb down it: you'd need a bulldozer to move all those rocks.

For more accessible amusement and natural beauty, continue driving north on winding **Highway 22**. Officially designated as a Scenic Byway by the state of North Dakota, this road leads you through butte-and-mesa country, only greener for much of the year than its southwest counterparts. Agriculture persists in the form of sunflowers, but as a whole the landscape suggests Western movies. Grays, purples, and rose-reds infest the rocks, themselves eroded into fanciful shapes. Locals have labeled some as the Three Old Maids and that perennial favorite, Eagle Rock, but you can make up your own names (or not). The slopes become steeper, the gullies more pronounced, and the round knobs of chalky bentonite that signify true badlands spread out before the traveler as you make your way up to ultra-scenic **Little Missouri State Park** (see *Best* *of North Dakota*). The park is geared to horseriders, but don't let that stop you if you're in a horseless carriage. From the parking lot, look down into a badlands paradise, where shallow streams slink to the nearby Little Missouri River and high ridges on the west suggest the Rockies, still hundreds of miles away. This uncrowded spot deserves more attention.

*Badlands view from Little Missouri State Park*

Also from Killdeer, you may proceed west and north on Highway 200, which incorporates U.S. Route 85 on the way to **Watford City**, another smallish burg reeling under the Bakken impact. Good news: the population influx has bumped Watford City's high school teams into a higher, more competitive bracket. Questionable news: the schools, along with all other government institutions, are bursting at the seams and much bond money will be needed to adequately serve all these new people.

**Be careful** when you drive Highway 85. Just as on U.S. 2 near, in and around Williston, pounding semis vie with road construction crews in making your travels slow, difficult and dangerous. Allow plenty of time, and expect delays, and keep your eyes peeled for hopped-up types who think they can drive on the shoulder or pass with impunity. The best choice for the traveler is to exit Route 85 before the Little Missouri and head west instead, into **Theodore Roosevelt National Park (North Unit)**.

TRNP is hands-down North Dakota's biggest draw, but you won't find typical national-park crowding here, especially at the North Unit. This is an unalloyed Good Thing, as the scenic drive that loops through this section of the park is of the amazing persuasion, even to those already jaded by Western natural splendors.

Sculpted smooth stone the colors of melted ice cream—vanilla, chocolate and strawberry—alternate with wide swaths of grassy meadow. Here as in nowhere else in the state there are Western trees like pine and juniper, tough trees that stand up to screeching winds, death-dealing lightning and the occasional avalanche. The ground falls away in a series of ripples, rounded and hairy with grass where it isn't eroded. Erosion, though, is the star of the badlands show.

**Theodore Roosevelt National Park (North Unit)**

Although there are no end of hiking and backpacking trails here and in the more popular South Unit, most travelers will opt for the 14-mile officially-designated Scenic Drive that leads from the park's entrance to Oxbow Overlook, where the Little Missouri's sinuous turns and great loops start bending south instead of west. **Don't miss this**: there are beautiful stretches of highway (as you surely know by now) throughout the state, but here is an area devoted to that beauty, sans farms, fields, oil rigs, Cold War pyramids or other distractions. The road stays on the north side of the river, hugging it in places and in others gliding up hills and skirting cliffs.

In the first few miles, don't be surprised if you see longhorn cattle: no, those horns are not fake, and no, you have not been accidentally beamed into the Fort Worth Stockyards. Teddy himself raised these mean-looking cows, and to this day they seem more horn and bone than potential hamburger and ribeye. Unless you really, really want an interesting story to tell at home and you have excellent health insurance, stay away from the longhorns, which are fast, unthinking and unpredictable.

Before long you come to something called the **Slump Rock Pullout** (the second pullout, not far from the longhorns). The park's brochure advises you that here, entire bluffs have slid from the clifftops, not as the result of avalanche or earthquake but simply because there was too much rock piled atop more rock that was too weak to support it. You can see this yourself, in your backyard with a water hose: make a mudpile, then plop more mud on top of it. As the mud dries, the topheavy segment will sag and eventually *slump* down beside the original pile.

It all looks more beautiful here, when shredded-fleece clouds spin by overhead and green grass caps the hills. Imagine yourself on a painted pinto pony (they still roam wild around here, although they are elusive and seldom seen), on your way back to the lodge after a successful hunt. You're thinking of savory buffalo tongue and a new robe, when all of a sudden eight to ten feet of supposedly solid earth crashes from the cliffs beside you, almost at your horse's feet. "Take it easy, Swift Lightning," you tell the frightened beast, but you hear your own voice shaking and your head is buzzing with questions about *how this might be*. Geological facts, as we know them today, remove the mysterious from these phenomena, but wouldn't it be more exciting and more fun to attribute this sudden collapse to an animal or an ancestral spirit? Now you have a story to tell. (Caveat: we do not know whether these slumps occurred in historical time, nor do Indian legends exist about them. Nice idea, though).

Gather up your shattered nerves and proceed to the **Cannonball Concretions Pullout**. You can't miss the formations that give their name to this place: they lie around everywhere, like giants' bowling balls. These strange spheres came to be when natural cements such as calcium carbonate began to coalesce around organic fragments like leaves and shells embedded in sediments, i.e. dirt or sand. Let's say you encased a leaf in concrete and then covered the concrete in dirt. In time, the dirt would wear away and the concrete would be exposed (don't try this at home – it could take a few hundred thousand years or so). Winds and other pressures would then whirl the concrete into a rounded shape like the ones you see here. Elsewhere in the state, these concretions are so common they're used as lawn ornaments.

*Cannonball concretions, popping out of bentonite*

There's a picnic area and a campground just after the pullout, on the banks of the River. The next big stop on the scenic drive is **Caprock Coulee Trail**. This is an easy self-guiding trail that wanders for 1.6 miles past coulees, or dry gulches, and breaks, or sudden drop-offs from the surrounding plains. At the **River Bend Outlook**, the Upper Coulee Canyon trail takes off to the north and intersects the Caprock Coulee Trail. Although the road past this point may be closed in the winter months, we're assuming you won't be there at that time and will continue to the **Bentonite Clay Overlook**, about ¾ of the way through the scenic drive. Bentonite is a fascinating substance, used in everything from toothpaste to candy bars to cosmetics. Its peculiar waxy texture makes it fun to climb on, but if you're there after a rain, be careful: wet bentonite feels greasy and is slippery, and ending up at the bottom of a hill covered in multicolored clay is probably not one of your vacation goals.

There are many other worthwhile destinations in the North Unit of TRNP, including the **Aschenbach Trail** that covers 17.7 meandering miles west to east across the park. On the way, you'll pass **Sperati Point** where the Little Missouri edges through its narrowest pass through the badlands. Hard to believe, but in ancient times the Little Missouri actually flowed north from here all the way to Hudson's Bay. Ice age glaciers eventually blocked that route, forcing the river to bust through the rocks right here.

By the way, the word "badlands" comes from the French, *mal pais*, and its use here reflects the voyageur's obsessions with forests and furs. There are no beavers here, no otter, mink or muskrat for that matter, and consequently the scrappy French gave these lands a pass. Their loss: places like this make the simply pretty look childish, provincial, more like a postcard than natural life. Badlands have a heart-filling majesty and strength that speaks to much that is inexpressible in us. They are immortal. They laugh at the passage of time. They resist comfort and convenience. They can be hard to access, hard to enjoy. And yet wise travelers sometimes echo the 20th century writer Oliver LaFarge: "I came to see the country with a rush, and to know that it was beautiful, and that I loved it." The TRNP badlands can still give you that rush.

When it's time to go, return south on U.S. 85 through the **Little Missouri National Grassland**, past the intersection with Route 200 all the way down to I-94. Take the freeway fifteen miles to **Medora** and the turnoff to **Theodore Roosevelt National Park, South Unit**.

## MEDORA

Medora bills itself as an authentic Old West village, but be warned: the original site was long abandoned when entrepreneur and corporate executive Harold Shafer took over in 1962 and "restored" it. Today Medora is a commercial enterprise masquerading as a small town, with cutesy shops and twee cafes along with a few overpriced and not very impressive lodging choices. Guided hikes and horseback rides may be booked here, not to mention tickets to a "frontier musical", but sensible visitors may choose to pass on Medora's cheesiness and head straight into the park. You may not agree with this assessment; thousands of visitors each year obviously don't (see *Medora, The Real Story*, below).

### Theodore Roosevelt National Park, (South Unit)

Soon after the visitor center, you'll see a broken field with five-inch piles of dirt scattered around and some furry little critters skittering here and there. Congratulations: you're at the first of several **Prairie Dog Towns** scattered throughout this part of the park. Of course you'll want to pile out of the car and photograph these rambunctious rodents. The "dogs" are by now so inured to tourists that they will pose for your pictures.

*A prairie dog shows off his classic good looks.*

There's a **Vista Point**, an **Overlook**, and **Cottonwood Campground and Picnic Area** a little further in on the 36-mile **Scenic Loop Drive**, with trails to more prairie dog towns and along Paddock Creek, a tributary of the Little Missouri, before you get to the **Saddle Horse Rides** pack station in Peaceful Valley along the bigger river.

The story here is **coal**, lots of it, visible as a black stripe along the cliffs and, until recently, actually burning in the rock. While North Dakota never became a coal-mining state like Pennsylvania or Wyoming, the dusky fuel has been accumulating here since before dinosaur days (see *Beulah*, above). You can pick up lumps of the stuff and examine it, although be sure to obey park rules and put it back where you found it, or you could face a heavy fine.

The bright crimson rock that crops up everywhere is called **scoria**, and represents Nature's own brickworks. Come again? Well, imagine if you put a rock in your oven and baked it at high heat (*don't*). As with the cannonball concretions, the dirt on the rock would fall away and what remains would turn blood-red. Here, a burning coal seam acted as the oven, and the result is coruscating color that goes well with summertime green and fall tans.

What ignited the coal? This writer found a lump of lignite coal (on private land), brought it home and tried igniting it with a barbecue lighter. Nothing happened, beyond a few feeble and momentary sparks. The semi-scientific conclusion, therefore, is that it takes a lot of heat to get coal going, but once lit, it stays lit.

One of the most scenic parts of this park's South Unit is the **North Dakota Badlands Overlook**. The uniformly rounded shapes, almost the same height, suggest a city of small hills, a Hobbiton of sorts just waiting for the Halflings to pop out and start digging vegetables. The effect isn't busy, however, any more than it is grand and imposing like the Grand Tetons. This is a pocket wilderness, a landscape of the unusual that, far from intimidating the visitor, seems to promise accessible adventure and easy rewards. Nevertheless, take the usual precautions and watch out for buffalo: much bigger than the essentially tame creatures one sees in Yellowstone Park, these bison mostly avoid people, even seeking out niches and ledges where no trails go. If provoked, however, they may charge and you could end up resembling a pancake. Always employ common sense.

**Coal Vein Trail**, near the eastern end of the scenic drive, is an excellent way to see almost all the park's phenomena on one easy walk. Scoria, slump blocks, cannonball concretions, prairie dogs and badland all make appearances here, and the walk itself features very little elevation gain and is suitable for almost any hiker.

# *MEDORA: THE REAL STORY*

While passing through this hucksterish hamlet, you'll see many plaques and restaurant placemats with fawning descriptions of the original founder the Marquis de Mores, a French nobleman who came here one step ahead of his creditors, and named the settlement after his dark-haired, New York-born wife.

Don't be taken in by those photos of the handsome, mustachio'd marquis. It's well documented that he was a disgusting bigot, spewing all sorts of hatred toward Jews, blacks and Indians. His mad spending triggered his own massive fail, and he snuck home in disgrace ten years after arriving.

In one of history's best ironies, the racist De Mores was eventually murdered by African tribes in the Sahara. *Sic semper moronis!*

*The Marquis de Mores: a mustache-twirling villain.*
*photo courtesy of wikicommons*

About forty miles south and west of TRNP, in aptly named Slope County, lies the highest point in North Dakota. **White Butte**, just south of Amidon, rises to 3506 feet, puny by Montana or California standards but worth seeing for its startling sharkfin shape and glittery feldspar sides. Bear in mind that, while the butte is surrounded by a National Grassland, it is itself on private property. Look for the donation box.

With a population of 1647, the nearby town of **Bowman** may not seem like much, but actually it's had a 2% population rise since 2000, and the median income has risen almost $10,000 since that year. Blame it on the Bakken.

Near here are semi- or full-fledged ghost towns like Haley, Haynes, Gascoyne and the Bowman-Haley Dam behind new Haley Lake. The Bakken is still calling, however, and so it's time for a jaunt back along the interstate to **Dickinson.**

## DICKINSON

This college town with many fun eateries and offbeat watering holes is prettier than Williston but growing just as fast. This area is younger, hipper (again, this is a relative term – don't expect Brooklyn), and has more of a real-world feeling to it than the emptier, spacier parts of the state. There's an original and still-functioning downtown. Every hotel and restaurant chain you can name is well represented here, with Ramadas butting up against Days Inns and Holidays nudging Hamptons all along the I-94 strip northeast of town. In the summer months, reservations are recommended.

**Sleep**

The **Wyndham Microtel** (1597 6th Avenue West, 456-2000) is fairly typical of the genre, so typical that it's hard to distinguish among all its near-clones on the same street. Once inside, however, the Wyndham provides ample proof of why it was selected as one of TripAdvisor's Certificate of Excellence Award winners in 2013. Spacious and comfortable, rooms at the Wyndham have window seats where it's fun to perch and watch vehicles on I-94 seemingly come and go from nowhere, as the seesawing topology rises to an infinity point. Cars and trucks vanish into the western clouds, or, going east, reappear as if from the void.

**Eat**

Although there's nothing remarkable about chain restaurants, the **Applebee's** in Dickinson (289 15th Street West, 227-8573) draws visitors in with its prompt service and lively bar. All sorts of boom-time stories are told here; come prepared to listen, and ask.

Things to do in Dickinson include a visit to the **Dakota Dinosaur Museum**, (200 West Museum Drive, 225-3466). While kids will get big-eyed over the stegosaurus skeleton and other specimens, this place has real appeal for rockhounds, as minerals are displayed to excellent effect in an adjacent black-lit room. This small museum is a local couple's labor of love, and you may get a chance to chat with them when you visit.

The **Dickinson Museum Center** is great fun on a rainy day or any other time. They have an extensive photography collection, showing the region's history in pictures and featuring portraits of people from three grizzled cowboys swilling beer, circa 1920 or so, to an insurance company bowling team from the 1950s, with employees, all female, looking sideways at the boss, who sits at the center with a bowling ball on his lap. Also part of the museum is **Prairie Outpost Park**, a permanent exhibit that includes a vintage railroad car, a store, a church, and three other buildings, moved from elsewhere to this site. Evocative and authentic, this open-air slice of history will intrigue visitors of all ages.

For a natural break, visit **Patterson Lake Recreation Area** southwest of town. Visitors flock here to swim in the lake and enjoy the clean beaches. Jet-skis and boats are permitted, as is fishing with the appropriate license. A hangout spot for the town's young people, Patterson Lake is also family-friendly and a good leg-stretching stop.

## BISMARCK

**Note: remember to set your clocks ahead one hour, from Mountain to Central time,** as soon as you pass Glen Ullin on I-94 east, on your way to Bismarck.

So why is North Dakota's capital named after a 19th century German general? Two words: money and railroads. Hopeful citizens honored Otto von Bismarck, the architect of a unified Germany according to some, a pitiless warmonger and militarist to others, because they thought he might throw some funds in the way of the Northern Pacific Railway, which was facing tough times in the 1880s. Nice try; didn't fly. There is no record of Bismarck or his country contributing any money to

American railroad interests.

The town moved on, not necessarily in the right direction. The first Legislature was marked by brazen corruption involving the Louisiana Lottery (never mind that Bismarck is not in Louisiana), and there were four governors inside six months. The town was so distinguished for its winner-takes-all, Wild West attitudes that one young boy, when told that an adult he knew had died, asked, "Did he get shot?" When told no, the boy then asked, "Well, was it whiskey?" Again came a no, but the youngster was disbelieving. "He can't be dead," cried the precocious stripling, "cuz' shooting and whiskey's the only way men ever die in Bismarck!" That boy, by the way, was the son of a newspaper editor.

Newspapers have always flourished in Bismarck, whose political philosophies have been known to deviate from the conservative policies in favor elsewhere in the state. The *Bismarck Tribune*, continuously published since 1873 and thus the state's oldest surviving newspaper, got the scoop of the century in 1876, when their reporter, Mark Kellogg, was "embedded" with the 7th Cavalry as they marched into Montana under General Custer. Kellogg did not survive the battle of the Little Bighorn – nor, of course, did Custer and over 200 of his men – but he took careful notes, and these were found on his corpse, safely tucked into a buckskin pouch.

Over time Bismarck's hills were flattened, its rivers contained, and in the 1930s North Dakota's first skyscraper was built and named the State Capitol. If the architecture makes you think of Eastern Europe and the Cold War, you are pretty much on target: the progressive politics that captivated Bismarck back in Depression times demanded a building that looked like a socialist fantasy. Even today, the capital appears lonely and a little freakish among all the three- and four-story office buildings that dot the capital.

Within the capitol complex is the gotta-see **North Dakota State Heritage Society Museum** (612 E. Boulevard Avenue, 328-2666) an attractive bit of modern architecture with no end of visitor-friendly exhibits on natural, historical and cultural topics. You can see costumes and artifacts used in Ghost Dances, those last gasps of Plains Indians resistance, or marvel at the skeleton of a mososaur, an enormous reptile that snapped and swam in prehistoric Lake Agassiz. The sweep of the horns on the Bison Latifrons skull may make you glad these intimidating creatures are extinct, while the Early North Dakota exhibit, with its antique soda-fountain and storefront reproductions, calls up images of a simpler time. There's just one problem here: **the museum is closed until November 2014**, for important structural renovations. In other words, the place leaks. A visit on a rainy/snowy October day revealed trash cans liberally sprinkled through the vestibule, catching drips and pours as they came in. All is not lost, however: visit the **bookstore**, which stays open regardless. Here is a fantastic collection of North Dakotiana, from commemorative volumes to maps to personal memoirs and histories to Louise Erdrich novels. Clerks are well-informed and love to chat, and on the right day they may slip you a freebie or two if you act sufficiently interested.

The Bismarck area is also home to an assortment of open-air cultural treasures.

## FORT ABRAHAM LINCOLN

Love him or hate him, General George Armstrong Custer looms large in North Dakota history. Just outside of Mandan is the place where he and his remarkably resilient bride, Elizabeth, lived for three years beginning in 1873. Daily life was dull in this then-isolated spot, but the Custers managed to install crystal chandeliers, hire bands, and hold dances that were as glittery as it was possible to be in North Dakota at that time.

One incident of those days that reverberated down the line was a conflict between Tom Custer, the general's brother, and the famous Sioux chieftain Rain-in-the-Face. Apparently RITF, as we shall call him, was going around bragging about killing two white men on a raid, and Tom Custer had him arrested and jailed at the fort. RITF pulled off a daring escape and hot-footed his way back to Sitting Bull's camp. Three years later, all the troops filed off in glittering array for Montana and, ultimately, the Battle of the Little Bighorn – where RITF claimed he killed Tom Custer personally and mutilated his body in a rather gruesome way.

Today, Fort Abraham Lincoln State Park (4480 Ft. Lincoln Rd., 667-6340) offers daily tours of the impressive, two-story white house and the adjoining Indian village (see below) from May through September. There's an attractive campground, picnic areas and a playground for kids, spread out over the gentle hills and bluffs overlooking the Missouri.

**On-A-Slant Indian Village**, named for its sloping location, contains lodges and lodge rings similar to those found at Knife River. Boardwalks and trails lace the area, and visitors may enter some lodges and gape at their spacious interiors and ingenious ventilation systems. There are no food concessions at the park, so remember to bring your own provisions.

If you have time, and if weather permits, continue south on Highway 1806. You'll be following Lewis & Clark's authenticated trail, but equally important will be your entry into the **Standing Rock Indian**

**Reservation**, a Sioux bastion that extends across the border into South Dakota. Sitting Bull College is here, offering graduate and undergraduate degrees. Listen to the local radio station's traditional music and tribe-oriented news, and look for the forlorn wooden sign that leads visitors into a mostly deserted parking lot and the alleged grave of America's most famous Indian chief. Sitting Bull was murdered at Fort Yates (while trying to surrender – or escape, depending on whom you ask) and there is good reason to believe that he was buried here. However, Mobridge, South Dakota has erected its own monument and claims the great man's bones for itself. Since this is a book about North Dakota, we'll stick to the opinion that Sitting Bull does lie here, under a concrete slab. A little more dignity might be appropriate for such an inspirational, if controversial, figure.

From **Cannon Ball**, located halfway between Mandan and Fort Yates, you could take Route 24 back to Highway 6, go north (right) on 6 and continue west on Highway 21. This is a quiet rural route that swings back toward some of the state's tiny German-Russian settlement towns. In **Regent**, you'll find the astonishing Gary Greff statues mentioned in "Best of North Dakota," at this book's beginning. The Cannonball River crosses the highway and meanders up to pretty **New England**, where West Rainy Butte rises to nearly 3400 feet. From here, it's only 24 miles north on Highway 22 back to I-94.

# GUINNESS WORLD RECORDS SET IN NORTH DAKOTA –

## THE BIG FOUR

### 1. Largest pot of chili ever made, Minto, 6/18/13

It took 170 volunteers in the northeastern town of Minto, but they did it, turning out 2,420 pounds of chili con carne to break the Guinness World Record for the largest single serving of chili. They cooked the red stuff in a 300-gallon milk container, and served it up on a sunny Tuesday in June. No word on the amount of antacids sold later in the vicinity.

### 2. Most simultaneous snow angels, Bismarck, 2/17/07

It's simple: just get on over to the state capitol grounds in Bismarck, drop onto your back in the snow, and commence waving your arms and legs. What may have looked like insanity or self-mortification paid off on February 17, 2007, when nearly nine thousand people – 8,962 to be exact – flopped down in the white stuff and windmilled away. At no other time had so many angels been created at the same time in the same place. That'll show 'em!

### 3. Longest ice cream sundae ever made, Cavalier, 6/9/12

Dixie cups? Sugar cones? So passé. What you want for your favorite summer treat is an aluminum roof gutter, 670 feet of it in all. Every four feet, drop in a gallon of ice cream and top it with nuts, fruit, fudge, etc. That makes for enough sundae to feed the entire town, wolfish kids and teenagers included. Once again, however, North Dakota was soon overshadowed by the bully to the east: White Bear, Minnesota broke this record one year later.

### 4. World's largest pancake breakfast, Fargo, 2/9/08

Carbs, cholesterol and sugar: happiness in North Dakota. The local Kiwanis Club came up with this project, livening up the winter scene by cooking and serving 34,818 pancakes within 8 hours, producing more sticky fingers than a glue factory.

**HONORABLE MENTION:** World's Largest Hamburger, Rutland, 1982. Our favorite small town built a special 16-foot frying pan for the occasion, and used a crane to flip the 3, 020-pound burger. Got buns?

# PART TWO: UNDERSTANDING THE STATE

## *GEOGRAPHY*

This part is easy. Flat in the east, rolling in the northeast, high plateaus in the northwest, mesas and badlands in the southwest. The Missouri River, dammed and ponded, enters North Dakota from the south in almost the middle of the state and flows north past Bismarck as far as Coleharbor in McLean County. Here, at the Garrison Dam, it becomes Lake Sakakawea and in this form continues to angle in a northwest direction until meeting up with the Yellowstone at Buford, on the Montana line.

It's impossible to underestimate the importance of the Missouri, or "Big Muddy" as it is sometimes affectionately called, to the development and atmosphere of North Dakota as a whole. As we will see in the "History" section, Lewis and Clark's winter at Mandan, and their cordial relations with the tribes living there, was essential to the success of their expedition and to the understanding of the entire West. The Missouri, which at that time was undammed and navigable throughout the state, provided a watery highway for traders, explorers and eventually settlers through this new, raw and intimidating country. Today the historic sites, recreational areas, state parks and wildlife refuges that cluster around its banks and bends draw vacationers of all stripes eager to see, learn and participate in our state's unique natural and cultural setting.

Grasslands are another crucial feature in the North Dakota landscape. From the Sheyenne in the east to the Little Missouri in the west, sections of land have been set aside to preserve the aboriginal mixed-grass and short-grass prairies that once supported hundreds of thousands of animals from buffalo and elk to prairie dogs and their nemeses, black-footed ferrets. To the casual observer, these grasslands aren't much to see: they lack the drama of the tall grass to the east, where a man on horseback could disappear, or the Rocky Mountains to the west. Flora fans will note, however, the different species of wildflowers that flourish here and bring hot pinks, burning yellows, smoldering reds and other colors to the landscape. Stand in the grasslands on a hot summer day and watch the wind (there is always wind) fondle and ripple the sea of stalks. You'll see why the prairie has so often been compared to an ocean, and you too may feel at sea, as your rental car floats with (we hope) serenity over the billowing green and yellow waves.

Badlands have been unfairly labeled. To desert fanciers, these eroded buttes and the rocky valleys that surround them are things of beauty to rival the reddest New England autumns or the palmiest Florida sands. Rising land and down-cutting rivers have created these seemingly random but in truth quite symmetrical lands, while wind and rain, those old reliables, have gone Michelangelo on the exposed surfaces, sculpting fanciful and suggestive shapes to rival anything further west. Perhaps the badlands' most surprising feature is their suddenness: twenty miles west of Dickinson, a bend is crossed and the freakiness appears. Also, unlike similar environments around the country, there is in spring and summer a fuzz of green growth over everything and always, there is a possibility of rain. Seeing the badlands backed by a lowering, purple sky, perhaps with the rumble of thunder adding an aural effect, can make you feel part of the landscape and enhance your experience the way a picture-perfect postcard view just can't.

Kettle lakes and glacial moraines, more Ice Age souvenirs, occur in the north and northeast. And everywhere, of course, there are the farmlands, spreading out alluvial fans, folding into coulees, rising on tilted slopes to the horizon or just drowsing next to their fringes of cottonwoods as if listening to the crops grow.

*Badlands*

## *GEOLOGY*

Houses sit on it. Farms grow on it. Highways traverse it and, yes, streams and rivers run through it. That dirt beneath your feet in North Dakota could be piano-black or rose-red, could be thick gray clay or fine powdery sand. Sometimes it's even ordinary brown loam.

What's important to remember is that land in North Dakota has been formed and shaped and changed by factors obvious and obscure, over hundreds of millions of years. In addition, the continent wasn't always where it is now. Back in dinosaur times, for example, what is now North Dakota nestled somewhere in the vicinity of the equator. Think hot, wet and muggy, something like today's Florida Everglades. As the supercontinent Pangaea moved north and broke up thanks to tectonic forces, associated changes swept across what would become the Plains. Much, much later came the Ice Ages that laid down glacial sheets from Hudson's Bay to southern Kansas and, in retreating, carved out hills and valleys and left behind boulders and lakes.

One of the most fascinating aspects of those ancient times was the Pierre Sea, a descendant of the Western Interior Seaway and a forerunner of Lake Agassiz, a shallow, not too salty ocean of sorts that at one time ran from the Arctic Ocean all the way to the Gulf of Mexico. Herein swam thirty-foot-long snapping lizards known as plesiosaurs or mososaurs, swift-swimming creatures with crocodile jaws and dinosaurian long necks. There were sea turtles too, sharks galore, squid and octopii, and bony fish not unlike today's gars. When these seas vanished, their sediments became the flatlands of the Red River Valley.

In the Tertiary Era, after that asteroid flopped into the Gulf of Mexico and ended the rule of the dinosaurs, small, oddly shaped mammals began to sniff and prowl the newly dry areas west of the present Missouri. The *ptilodon*, squirrel-bodied with an opossum-like tail, and the *hesperocyon*, which had doglike teeth and appetites but looked more like a meerkat or mongoose, darted around the plains and hid from predators like *dinictis*, the saber-toothed cat. Horses the size of piglets scampered here and there, camels and llamas sedately trotted by, and giant sloths (hairy possums on steroids) slouched towards waterways or munched tall grasses.

All that changed when the ice sheets began to move. Then we had the woolly mammoths with the long, curling tusks, the American mastodon that resembled the Indian elephant, the dire wolves three times bigger than today's *Canus lupus*, and the fascinating long-horned bison that frequented forests and wooded areas, unlike our more familiar (and also smaller) buffalo of the open prairie. By the end of these days, approximately 10,000 years ago, native Americans were hunting down these creatures and etching their likenesses into stones, along with those of mythical beings like the thunderbirds depicted on Writing Rock in Divide County near the Montana line.

In today's North Dakota, geological wonders are both visible and buried, but not inaccessible to the curious tourist. **At Theodore Roosevelt National Park, for instance, adults and kids can pay to go**

**on one-day digs,** ferreting out bones and teeth of long-extinct species under the guidance of professional paleontologists. For half the price of one night in a Williston chain motel, you might unearth the jaw of a *hyaenodon*, a mammal with leopardlike spots and tail, a donkey's short mane, and the head of an enormous and bad-tempered dog.

*Hyaenodon*
*courtesy of wikipedia*

# HISTORY & SETTLEMENT

## NATIVE AMERICANS

Sometime around 18,000 years ago a band of people stood shivering on an empty plain. To the east, where the sun came up, lay a wall of ice five feet high and several miles wide. Bluish-white, with water trickling from its peaks and pooling in its crevices, the ice sheet kept these people cut off from its far sides, although they could travel west and south without impediment. They bore sharpened sticks and spear-throwers to be used on their prey, and knives for flaying the hides of the great brown beasts that roamed in seemingly infinite herds over the prairies.

The Paleo-Indians in North Dakota left little record of their passage. At Lake Ilo in Dunn County, scientists found one of their campsites, and at Alkali Creek in Williams County, in the heart of the oil-shale boom, the Indians apparently maintained a workshop where they made stone tools out of native flint. Not much is known about these first North Dakotans. They may have hunted mammoths, mastodons, and other Ice Age mammals, although there is no proof of that as yet. As the last Ice Age waned and the glaciers shrank, the climate became warmer. Streams dried up and became meadows, removing water sources for the great beasts. The bison, however, was able to adapt, shrinking in size and developing smaller horns, and they became the dominant grass-eaters on the plains.

Among the first modern Indian tribes in the Dakotas were the Arikaras, a river-centered culture that had split off from the Caddos and Pawnees to the south. Friendly with larger tribes such as the Mandan and Hidatsa, the Arikaras grew corn, beans and squash, perhaps learning the cultivation of these foods from more southerly peoples such as the Hopi and Pueblos. In the summer, men hunted buffalo while women tended the garden plots.

Before the Europeans came, the Mandan and Hidatsa were beyond doubt the most important prairie tribes. Despite some cultural differences between them, the two peoples lived together in large villages, where they built comfortable earth lodges and shared food. They traded with other Indians from as far away as New Mexico and Tennessee, and were among the first to negotiate with French fur trappers and English military men who came down from Canada.

In the 1830s, a smallpox epidemic decimated the North Dakota tribes. From almost four thousand people, their numbers shrank to barely 1,200.

Although, contrary to legend, the Mandan and Hidatsa were not deliberately infected by the white man, a combination of poor living conditions, an unbalanced diet, exposure to previously unknown domestic animals and a lack of antibodies to this and other infectious diseases contributed to the tragically high death rate. In 1862, the Mandan, Hidatsa and Arikara chose to combine themselves into the Associated Tribes. They agreed to live at Fort Berthold, in Montrail County, after refusing to move to Oklahoma.

Today once again there are approximately 1,200 Mandan, and their language has been revived and is being taught in elementary schools. Although their communal life was disturbed by the building of the Garrison Dam in the 1950s, the Three Tribes continue proud of their heritage and hopeful of their future.

The Mandan language is a Siouxian dialect, and the Dakota branch of the Sioux nation gave their name to a vast territory. At one point, Sioux ranged all the way up to the Heart River in Morton County, and there were numerous encounters, most of them bloody, with the Three Tribes. Having no patience for agriculture and already seething at the Europeans who had driven them west from Minnesota and Wisconsin, the Sioux did not suffer interference with their traditional ways (even though some of these traditions, such as nomadism and hunting from horseback, dated back only a few hundred years).

Standing Rock, a Lakota reservation, straddles the North-South Dakota line, and travelers heading north on U.S. 83 can tune in to a local station that broadcast tribal chants and call-in shows in Siouxan languages. Listening to the undecipherable speech, any imaginative traveler can picture the land as it once was, when the humped, rounded shapes in the fields were not bales of hay but buffalo. Sitting Bull College is here, and the great chief himself is buried on the reservation, on the banks of the Missouri.

There were many other Indian tribes who made their homes in the state and still live here today. Curious readers should investigate the Metis, a mixed-race offshoot of the Pembina and Red Lake Ojibwa, who today live mostly in the state's extreme northeast, along the Red River.

**First Europeans**

Once upon a time in Scotland, there lived a man named Thomas Douglas. Ordinary name, you say? Perhaps, but since most people knew him as the Fifth Earl of Selkirk he led a far from ordinary life. Disturbed by the wretchedness of crofters, or small tenant farmers, in his native country, Selkirk managed to acquire 116,000 acres of Red River Valley land and in 1816 he founded the first European settlement in North

Dakota.

Woops. The Metis, armed by white agents of the Northwest Company, wiped out the tiny colony in 1817, but after Selkirk himself came to the place, the former Scotsmen and women returned and the settlement, called Fort Daer, thrived.

Well before then, however, what is now North Dakota had witnessed one of the most unlikely yet influential phenomena in American history. We're talking, of course, about Lewis and Clark, whose expedition among other things was charged with the task of meeting the Mandan and Hidatsa, establishing trade between them and the newly-hatched United States, and learning from them all there was to know about the country to the West. Unfortunately for Meriwether L. and his red-headed buddy Bill, the Three Tribes were unable or unwilling to let the explorers in on the continent's biggest secret, i.e. the size, scale and extent of the Rocky Mountain chain.

In the fall of 1804, after a largely uneventful trip up the Missouri from St. Louis, the explorers wandered into what is now Fort Mandan and received a warm welcome from the assorted Indians. They built their own fort but socialized extensively with the Three Tribes, introducing them to Christmas and New Year's Eve celebrations and amusing them with dancing and music provided by expedition fiddler Pierre Cruzatte. The Indians were particularly bemused by Lewis' Newfoundland dog, Seaman, whom they believed to be a god until they saw him mating with one of their own spotted dogs.

They were equally intrigued by York, Clark's servant, the first African-American they had ever seen, and he patiently put up with their questions and attentions, many of which might seem rude today.

*Bison Dance of the Mandan, as painted from life by George Catlin*
*photo courtesy of wikicommons*

Tucked between buffalo skins and chowing down on puppy-dog stew, Lewis and Clark were in turn impressed with the Three Tribes. The Mandan and Hidatsas profited from trade with all the Indians downstream on the Missouri, and handled goods that flowed in from the High Plains and mountain tribes. At times, of course, these goods were people, and they did not so much flow in as they were kidnapped during raids and hauled against their will over hundreds of miles, often across the back of a horse. Among these unwilling denizens was one Sakakawea, a Shoshone from the Rockies. Snapped up by the Hidatsa in a jolly springtime raid that killed her mother and most of her family, the eleven-year-old girl lived sullenly among her captors until she caught the eye of one Charbonneau ("Sharbono" and worse, according to Clark's journals), a French-Canadian trapper and indifferent linguist who married her at fifteen.

She was already pregnant when her forty-something husband, useless in boats, an unhappy camper but a master *charcoutier* who could do wonders with a buffalo's intestines, signed onto the expedition that would head west in April, 1805. You can learn a great deal more about the Corps from many sources, but I recommend above all a work of fiction, *I Should Be Extremely Happy in Your Company*, by Brian Hall. This absorbing novel takes us inside the minds of the leaders, of Charbonneau and of Bird Woman herself. It's a literary tour de force, far more gripping than a footnote-laden biography or snoozefest public-TV documentary.

Not for children, however.

*SAKAKAWEA – Teenaged mom who won the West.*
*photo courtesy of wikicommons*

The Europeans who were destined to made North Dakota their permanent home, however, were for the most part not Anglo-Saxon by birth. We will tell their stories in the next section.

# THE NORWEGIANS

To the casual channel-surfer landing on a *Globe Trekker* episode or a National Geographic special, Norway looks like a beautiful country. Majestic mountains, deep blue fjords, charming wooden villages and centuries of folklore – why would anybody want to leave this paradise?

People are funny, though. They like to eat. More to the point, they need to eat, and Norway's rocky, thin-ribbed pastures were just about tapped out in the mid-nineteenth century. Worse still, the country's law declared that only eldest sons could inherit land, a ridiculous statute which happily had much to do with the development of the United States. Younger sons and strong-minded daughters seethed in frustration, both at this law and at the ancient monarchy that ruled the land. Many came to feel, as did Ole Rolvaag's protagonist in his masterly novel *Giants in the Earth*, that "no old, worn-out, thin-shanked, pot-bellied king" should be running their lives. America – the *goldene medina* to the Jews, the Gold Mountain to the Chinese, *el norte* today – sang its syncopated siren song to embittered farmers, rednosed fishermen, cranky carpenters and just about everyone else in old *Norge*. Sensible, practical, slow to anger and in most cases deeply religious, Norwegians began to pack up and head for the wharves. After all, thanks to Leif Ericksson whose Vikings briefly colonized what is now Canada's east coast, they did preceded Columbus on this continent by some three hundred years.

Always a literate people, Norwegians devoured letters sent home by the first pioneers. You can easily imagine the stunned looks and rapid thinking that must have been provoked by passages like these, written by immigrants in Wisconsin around 1849. "They have more respect for girls here than in Norway. When an American wants to hire a maid, he comes with a horse and carriage …"

Really? Respect for *girls*? Prospective maids riding in carriages?

A stronger inducement for a king's reluctant subjects came in this passage. "Here it is so that a working man will never be [barred[ from the husband's or master's table to eat, whether he works for a shopkeeper or others. All shall be as highly respected. Yes, Americans are friendly and high-flightedness we cannot understand. We are so used to the proud Europeans who are haughty …"

This was intoxicating stuff, and as the folks at home reached for the *akavit* and a crust of bread with herring, the conversation must have taken some extraordinary turns.

The attraction of Norwegians to North Dakota isn't hard to understand. Having broken their backs on rocky slopes, they yearned above all for flat, stonefree land that was cheap if not free. The American Homestead Act, a piece of legislation that enriched the nation to the nth degree, enabled even penniless immigrants to settle up to 640 acres of land. If, in seven years, they had "proved up" the land by staying on it and building permanent structures, the claim was theirs. The cost? Fourteen dollars to register the claim, and all the blood, sweat, toil and tears a family could generate while working eighteen-hour days. In winter, ropes were tied between houses and barns after settlers blinded in white-out blizzards perished fifty yards from their hearths. In spring, adhesive mud collected on horses' hooves and wagons' underpinnings, making effective travel nearly impossible. Locusts were common around harvest time, with the Ten Plagues reference not lost on these bible-reading people. In midsummer, of course, there was the usual onslaught of blood-sucking mosquitoes that tortured men and beasts alike.

Yet they stayed, and they prospered. Today North Dakota boasts the largest percentage of Norwegian-Americans in the U.S., at 55%. When you think of other immigrant groups that have been whittled away over the generations by intermarriage, wanderlust and competing ideologies, this statistic is impressive.

When in North Dakota, ask around. Norwegians are notorious coffee-drinkers, and after a strong cup or two these normally taciturn men and women may well turn loquacious. There's a great pride to be taken in making the desert bloom, even if that desert is covered in snow half the year and flooded each spring. The stories may be old, but they are still true, and worth hearing.

*Norwegian pioneers with their sod house in North Dakota*

## GERMAN-RUSSIANS

Many years ago this writer met a young man in Iowa City who spoke with a pronounced South German accent. Always a show-off (I was young too, and he was very handsome), I sprang some of my best *Deutsch* on him, absorbed around the kitchen table from my refugee father and his German-speaking siblings. To my surprise, the young man shook his head. "I don't shpik German."

"You don't? But I – "

He smiled, displaying dazzling teeth. "I'm vrom Norse Dakotta," he said, as if that explained everything.

That was my first introduction to the German-Russians, a little known people from an obscure land who were to much of southern North Dakota what the Norwegians were to the state north of Grand Forks. Unlike the Norwegians, whose king annoyed but did not actively oppress them, the German-Russians sought religious as well as economic freedom in America, and they proved less eager to learn English and assimilate.

It all started with Catherine the Great. Of German origin herself, this 18th century Russian tsarina saw that Russian serfs and their masters were not producing enough food and taking sufficient advantage of fertile lands around the Black Sea shores. In a strange parallel to the American immigrant experience a century and a half later, Germans summoned by Catherine trudged across the hills and vales of eastern Europe, many settling in Ukraine where native people, Muslim Tatars and perplexed Jews had made their home for centuries.

Ukraine was good practice for North Dakota. Here the Eurasian steppe stretched flat as far as eye could see, and trees were few. Here harsh winters gave way to hot summers, and the soil produced wheat, hay, potatoes and other crops in abundance. The Germans' strong work ethic and comparative sobriety helped them gain an edge on their ethnic Russian and Ukrainian neighbors, and for many years they prospered while maintaining their native language, their religion (mostly Roman Catholic), their music and culture. They also weren't drafted into Russian armies, as stipulated by Catherine the Great and hewed to by successive tsars – up to a point.

The point was Tsar Alexander II, who ascended to the throne in 1855. Alexander instituted many reforms, including freeing the serfs, but he had an innate distaste for foreigners. Soon the German-Russians found themselves facing a series of onerous laws that will sound sadly familiar to students of 20th century history. They could not practice their faith, attend universities, or even speak their language in public. Compulsory military service was expected, and enforced. Locals were encouraged to harass the communities. Heads were broken and innocents jailed, or worse. In 1872, the German-Russians started leaving, and they left in droves. In kerchiefs and flat caps, with wide aprons and hobnailed boots, they crowded the shores of Ellis Island. Like the Norwegians, they had no intention of remaining in the urban East.

They poured into North Dakota, settling for the most part east of the Missouri and south of Highway 2. They built sod houses, where the grass on the roof served as cover for snakes and dust rained down day and night. More clannish than Norwegians, they stayed on their farms as if glued to the land. Improvements came slowly, if at all. Outhouses were common before World War II. Electricity was rare; what for? They made their own candles and used kerosene lamps. They built icehouses, or preserved food underground.

A musical people, the German-Russians made their own instruments and kept up the traditional songs of the old country. Girls stayed at home, and boys left school early. News of the outside world seldom penetrated the sod huts and, later, the stout wooden farmhouses that rose over the plains. Tiny churches, often standing alone in a field, resounded with hymns every Sunday, and passers-by sniffed with appreciation the odors of *strudel*, of black bread, and of *galupsi*, or stuffed cabbage, that wafted from well-scrubbed windows.

As more children insisted on going to high school, or even college, the framework of German-Russian life in North Dakota began to sag like the abandoned barns you see today off Highway 83. North Dakota's German-Russian population is still high, but today the great-grandchildren of pioneers are often professionals, tending the sick, educating the young, defending their neighbors in court or tackling the tax code.

The change did not always come easily. Famous North Dakotan Lawrence Welk, who never lost his German accent, left his family at nineteen for the glamour of a musical career. Although Americans of a certain age will remember Welk's toothy grin and merry accordion on TV every Saturday night, not too many people these days beat a path to the Lawrence Welk birthplace, a restored farmhouse near Strasburg in Emmons County. The "King of Champagne Music," who earned a star on the Hollywood Walk of Fame, never went back himself.

*He never went home again: Lawrence Welk*
*courtesy of rednecklatte.com*

# HUTTERITES

They aren't Amish, nor are they Mennonite. They wear black hats, don't watch TV, have huge families and stick strictly to the teachings of a charismatic leader, but they're not Hasidic Jews either. They celebrate Christmas, employ modern medicine, have no trouble owning farm machinery and do business on a vast scale, while eating and living communally and paying no wages to their members. They don't pay income tax or collect Social Security, yet they are not a tax-exempt religious organization. They forbid military service and the wearing of uniforms, including policemens' or fire fighters'. Women don't hold public office, and a trip away from home must be okayed by the governing body. These aren't Martians we're discussing here – they're Hutterites, and their seven communities, or "colonies" as they prefer, in North Dakota have been ongoing for over a hundred years.

Jacob Hutter, the 16th century founder of the movement, preached simplicity and cooperation. From their origins in Germany, Hutterites moved to Moravia and eventually to Russia, with several colonies in the Ukraine. However, they are not part of the German-Russian group despite their shared geographical and linguistic similarities. Hutterites are anabaptists, meaning that they don't baptize babies, but adults who have found their faith can be baptized anytime. In other respects, their theology is similar to that of many Protestant Christian sects. The New Testament is their primary text.

You can recognize Hutterites in North Dakota if you know their distinguishing signs. Men and boys today may wear cowboy hats and boots, but they eschew belts, favoring wide suspenders instead. Women wear black nunlike wraps that cover most of their hair, and long skirts. Don't expect bikinis or tank tops in Hutterite country. Vertically striped shirts are favored by men, while boys may wear a semi-stovepipe black cap with serious not-this-century cred. Although teenage Hutterites may leave the colony without dire consequences, some ninety percent of them return to resume their idyllic pastoral life.

Today most Hutterite colonies are in Canada, but they maintain seven in North Dakota, mostly in the southeast. Unassuming and matter-of-fact, the Hutterites have managed to fit into North Dakota society, although female life expectancy is lower than male and mental illness is far more likely to occur among Hutterite women than among men. Overall, the Hutterites are an extremely law-abiding and peaceful community. There has been not one murder – not one – in a Hutterite colony for over 400 years.

In North Dakota, Hutterites grow grain crops including wheat, oats, canola, flax, corn and barley. Typical Hutterite farms are comparatively smaller, and a Hutterite colony consists of forty families. Each family gets a room in a longhouse, rather than a house of their own, and upon marriage a young man must grow a beard. Divorce is a non-event; it just doesn't happen. Children are considered adults at 15 and while today they may continue in high school until graduation, the colony assigns jobs to 15 year olds, and they are expected to continue in these occupations throughout life.

Yes, they drive cars, and trucks. However, the colony owns the vehicles, as they own all farm equipment, housing and food. In practice, Hutterite ascetism, or willingness to do without luxury and material goods, is somewhat flexible and depends in many ways upon the individual. Generally, however, it's safe to assume that Hutterite women and girls don't have much leeway in what they do or how they behave.

Fascinating as Hutterites are, don't count on sharing their table, or their hospitality, anytime soon. Although they welcome salespeople and government workers – two species not much loved by the populace as a whole – in North Dakota they forbid tourist visits. Go figure.

*A Hutterite schoolroom*
*courtesy of Wikicommons*

# ACKNOWLEGMENTS/
# RECOMMENDED READING

Please visit our website, *www.NorthDakotaCurious.com*, for more information. We welcome your feedback! If there is anything in this book that is outdated, inaccurate, or just plain wrong, please contact us and we'll try to fix the problem.

Also on our website, you'll find additional photos, news, a blog, and much more. Feel free to send your own North Dakota stories and images to our Reader Feedback section.

This book could not have been written without the help of North Dakotans living and dead, whose stories, anecdotes, illustrations and considerable humor pointed me in directions ordinary research can't go. Specifically, I'd like to thank several North Dakota County Commissioners who responded to query letters from a total stranger and who took the time to meet with me and answer endless (and at times clueless) questions.

**Hetty Walker** of Pembina County provided detailed historical and contemporary information about her town and county. An indefatigable former war bride from the Netherlands, Ms. Walker took the author and her husband on a guided tour of the Pembina State Museum and also led us to a historic church: first it was Icelandic, then it was Ukrainian, now it's a community center.

**Rod Burgad** of Macintosh County met us for coffee in Wishek and showed us around downtown. He filled us in on farming and ranching practices in the area, discussed the many ways folks on the land make ends meet, and shared his knowledge of German-Russian cuisine and culture.

**Bill Anderson** of Sargent County went above the call of courtesy in showing us the town of Rutland and its environs. Although Bill's vision is limited subsequent to Agent Orange exposure in Vietnam, he is an avid computer user and a one-man repository of all things Sargent County. Thanks to Bill, we met his brother, wine-growing advocate **Paul Anderson**, and spent two nights at the Coteau de Prairie Lodge, where host **Joe Breker** showed us his farm and put up with my saying "Astonishing!" around 12,000 times.

Other helpful North Dakotans included **Edwin Olson**, sales manager at the John Deere store in Bottineau, who contributed greatly to our understanding of farm equipment; **Linda**, a particularly helpful ticket-taker at Bonanzaville; the **quilters** attending a convention in Fargo; and **Kathy Deckert**, a fun-loving gal we met at Minot's Hostfest whose late husband owned supposedly worthless land in the Bakken ... that is no longer worthless.

Thank you to Scott and Sahara of PandN Graphics for their work on the cover.

Thanks to Lee at IRONHORSE Formatting for helping us bring this book into being.

Thank you to Valerie Root for the use of her quilt. (www.EveningInTheGarden.wordpress.com)

"Thank you to our neighbor, Mandy Shames, for letting us photograph her UND jacket."

Numerous web sites, books, and pamphlets provided vital information. Some of the most outstanding sources were **ndtourism.org**, the state's own comprehensive tourism website (they also publish an excellent brochure); **ghostsofnorthdakota.com**, where a book as well as the website furnished invaluable facts and images, **roadsidend.com**, a place for all things offbeat and often overlooked, and **realnd.com**, another labor of love assembled by locals for everyone.

Not easy to get, but not impossible, was *North Dakota: A Guide to the Northern Prairie State*, published in 1938 as part of the WPA Writer's Program. While a Federal program for unemployed writers seems like a pipe dream today, it wasn't so in the Depression years, when groups of journalists, novelists, academics and others came together to craft this invaluable book. Furnished with black-and-white illustrations, the original *Guide* is a priceless artifact, providing a detailed look of how the state came together and where it stood before World War II.

Numerous works of fiction also contributed to the writing of this book. I've mentioned them before, but the novels of **Louise Erdrich** are essential to an understanding of the delicate relationship between white and native North Dakotans – and they're gorgeously written as well, and at times very funny. **Brian Hall**'s *I Should Be Extremely Happy in Your Company* presents Lewis, Clark, Sakakawea, Charbonneau and other members of the Corps of Discovery in their own voices. It is a moving, often wrenching retelling of the three-year journey, sometimes raunchy and graphic, sometimes transcendent and soaring, but always mindful of Meriwether Lewis' precarious mental state and its consequences. Although his books take place in eastern Colorado, **Kent Haruf** writes with majesty and lyricism about farmers, ranchers, drifters and others on the High Plains. *Plainsong*, perhaps his best novel, puts the reader squarely in the center of this life, and goes as far or farther than any factual book in evoking the peculiar harsh beauty of this area, which extends well into North Dakota.

Speaking of fiction, if you enjoyed the writing style in this travel guide you might be interested in reading my novel, *1989*, coming soon to your favorite online retailer. That book has absolutely nothing to do with North Dakota; it's the story of four ordinary L.A. suburbanites whose lives are changed by tumultuous events they see on television. Remember the Berlin Wall? These people won't forget about it soon.

There are many – too many – other people, places and things that have made this book a reality, but there's no way I would be writing this today without the help, love and support of my husband, **Dr. Isadore Wendel**. As traveling companion, photographer, co-researcher, and patient reader of my many drafts, he has no peer, and never will have.

**SYLVIA WENDEL**
**Los Angeles, California**
**March 6, 2014**

Made in the USA
Las Vegas, NV
24 February 2021